Music for Study

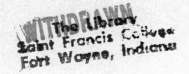
Music for Study
A Source Book of Excerpts

Second Edition

HOWARD A. MURPHY

ROBERT A. MELCHER
The Conservatory of Music
Oberlin College

WILLARD F. WARCH
The Conservatory of Music
Oberlin College

PRENTICE-HALL, INC., Englewood Cliffs, New Jersey

Library of Congress Cataloging in Publication Data

MURPHY, HOWARD ANSLEY
  Music for study.

  1.—Harmony. I.—MELCHER, ROBERT A., joint author.

II.—WARCH, WILLARD F., joint author. III—Title.
MT50.M98M9–1973   781.3   72–8776
ISBN 0–13–607515–0

© 1973 by Prentice-Hall, Inc.
Englewood Cliffs, New Jersey

Printed in the United States of America

10 9 8 7 6 5 4 3 2 1

PRENTICE-HALL INTERNATIONAL, INC., London
PRENTICE-HALL OF AUSTRALIA, PTY. LTD., Sydney
PRENTICE-HALL OF CANADA, LTD., Toronto
PRENTICE-HALL OF INDIA PRIVATE LIMITED, New Delhi
PRENTICE-HALL OF JAPAN, INC., Tokyo

Contents

v

3
The IV Chord, 11

4
The Cadential I$^6_4$ Chord, 16

5
The II and II$_6$ Chords, 20

6
The I$_6$, IV$_6$, and V$_6$ Chords, 25

9

The VI and VI₆ Chords, 45

10

The III and III₆ Chords, 52

11

The VII and VII₆ Chords, 57

15

The VII₇ Chord and Its Inversions, 78

16

Other Seventh Chords, 84

17

Secondary Dominants, 92

Section A: of V, 92

Section B: of IV, 94

18

Diminished Seventh Chords: Dominant Function, 105

23

Modulation to Other Closely Related Keys, 131

24

The Neapolitan Chord, 141

25

Augmented Sixth Chords, 148

28

Polychords and Polytonality, 177

29

Twelve-Tone Technique, 181

Supplementary Excerpts, 188

Introduction

The success of the first edition of *Music for Study* (by Murphy and Melcher, Prentice-Hall, 1960) has proved the need for a source book of musical excerpts to accompany courses in Music Theory.

The material is designed to parallel the harmonic vocabulary of college theory courses, and is arranged in accordance with general teaching practice rather than in agreement with any specific text. The excerpts, which range in length from four measures to complete compositions, have been selected to illustrate specifically one or more points of musical composition. Harmonic, melodic, rhythmic and formal elements are represented, as well as a wide variety of composers, periods, styles and media. In addition to analysis, these excerpts are useful for sight singing, sight playing, transposition, score reading and ear training.

This second edition follows the same format as the first, and includes many of the same excerpts. But the following changes have been made:

1. New excerpts have replaced certain previous ones in order to give new or clearer emphasis to certain elements of musical construction.
2. Sixteen Bach chorales (either in part or in whole) have been included.
3. Eight new chapters have been added to expand the harmonic vocabulary through the most frequently used chromatic chords, and to illustrate some of the most important techniques employed in the earlier part of the twentieth century.

The authors hope that this collection of excerpts from great music will bring to students a realization of the practical values of the study of Music Theory and will develop in them a deeper understanding and appreciation of the construction of fine music.

We deeply regret that Howard A. Murphy's untimely death in 1962 denied us the privilege of his valuable contributions to this second edition.

Robert A. Melcher
Willard F. Warch

Acknowledgments

The authors are grateful to Harold B. Bryson, Emeritus Professor of Singing and Frederick C. Gersten, Associate Professor of Singing, both of the Oberlin Conservatory of Music; and to Joseph R. Reichard, Professor of German, and Lawrence A. Wilson, Professor of French and Italian, both of the Oberlin College of Arts and Sciences, for their help in the translation of French, German, and Italian texts of the choral and vocal excerpts.

In addition, the authors are indebted to the publishers for permission to quote from the following material:

Boosey & Hawkes, Inc., New York: Verdi, *La Forza del Destino*
International Music Co., New York: Fauré, *Piano Quartet*; Verdi, *Falstaff*
Theodore Presser Co., Bryn Mawr, Pa.: *Analytic Symphony Series:*
    Beethoven, "Symphony III"; Brahms, "Symphonies I, III and IV"; Dvořák, "Symphony IX"; Mozart, "Symphonies in G Minor and E-flat Major"; Schubert, "Symphonies VII and VIII"; Schumann, "Symphony IV"; Sibelius, "Symphony I"; Tchaikovsky, "Symphonies IV and V"; Franz, *Marie*
G. Schirmer, Inc., New York: Caldara, *Alma del Core*; Chopin, *Mazurka*, Op. 59, No. 2; *Nocturnes:* Op. 15, No. 2 and Op. 37, No. 1; Mozart, *The Magic Flute*; Schubert, *Hedge Roses* and *Sonatina for Violin and Piano*, Op. 137, No. 3; Schumann, *An den Sonnenschein* and *Dichterliebe*; Verdi, *Il Trovatore* and *La Traviata*.

Acknowledgment of permission to use other copyrighted music will be found in the text where the material appears.

1

The I Chord
and Nonharmonic Tones

1. Beethoven (1770—1827), *Six Variations,* Op. 76

2. Mozart (1756—1791), *Piano Sonata in F Major,* K. 547a

3. Mozart (1756—1791), *Trio in B—flat Major,* K. 502

4. J.S. Bach (1685–1750), *Suite in E Major*

5. Tchaikovsky (1840–1893), *Symphony V,* Op. 64

Andante cantabile, con alcuna licenza

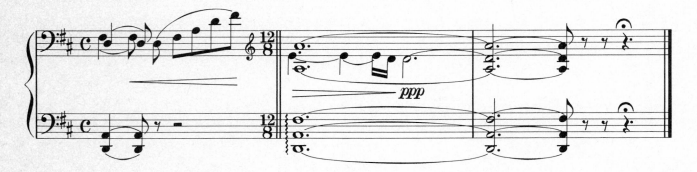

6. Verdi (1813–1901), *Il Trovatore,* Act IV, No. 19

Allegro agitato

Tu ve - drai che a-mo - re in ter - ra   mai del   mio   non fu   più for - te;
You shall   see   that of   earth's loves   none than   mine   has been   more ar - dent;

7. Smetana (1824—1884), *String Quartet in E Minor**

* To facilitate reading, this passage has been arranged for piano.

8. Chopin (1810–1849), *Nocturne,* Op. 15, No. 2

* The symbol ⌐ ⌐ indicates that the excerpt begins with the end of the preceding phrase or closes with the beginning of the following phrase.

2

The V, V₇ and V₉ Chords

9. Wagner (1813–1883), *The Flying Dutchman,* Overture

10. Schumann (1810–1856), *Album for the Young,* Op. 68, No. 12

11. Haydn (1732–1809), *Symphony in E–flat Major,* No. 103

12. Haydn (1732—1809), *Piano Sonatina IV in F Major*

13. Beethoven (1770—1827), *Trio,* Op. 1, No. 3

14. Schubert (1797–1828), *Die schöne Müllerin,* Op. 25, No. 2

15. Verdi (1813–1901), *La Traviata,* Act III, No. 16

so - gni_____ ri_____ den_____ ti, le ro - se_____ del_____
dreams and_____ of_____ love-ly smiles,_____ the ros - es_____ of_____ de -

vol - to_____ già_____ so - no_____ pal - len_____ ti;
sire_____ are al - read - y_____ fad - ed;_____

16. Schubert (1797–1828), *Waltz,* Op. 18a, No. 5

Reprinted from Peters Edition No. 150, Schubert *Tänze,* by permission of the publisher, C. F. Peters Corporation, 373 Fourth Avenue, New York 16, N.Y.

17. Beethoven (1770—1827), *Piano Sonata,* Op. 31, No. 2

18. Chopin (1810—1849), *Étude,* Op. 10, No. 3

19. Beethoven (1770–1827), *Sonata for Violin and Piano, Op. 24*

Adagio molto espressivo

3

The IV Chord

20. Chopin (1810—1849), *Nocturne,* Op. 37, No. 1

21. Verdi (1813—1901), *La Forza del Destino,* Act IV

Le mi - nac - cie, i fie - ri ac - cen ti, por - tin se - co in pre - da i
All your threats and proud de - fy - ing, to the winds un - heard are

ven - ti, per-do-na-te-mi pie - tà, O fra-tel, pie-tà, pie - tà.
fly - ing, show me pi - ty and for - give, bro - ther, pi - ty and for - give.

22. Dvořák (1841—1904), *Slavonic Dance,* Op. 46, No. 3

Allegretto scherzando

p

23. Brahms (1833—1897), *Symphony III,* Op. 90

Andante

p   *p*   *p*

I_6 I_6

24. Handel (1685—1759), *Messiah,* No. 44

Allegro

S.
A.

ff

Hal-le - lu - jah! Hal-le-lu-jah! Hal-le - lu-jah! Hal - le - lu - jah!

T.
B.

I_6

25. Schumann (1810—1856), *An den Sonnenschein,* Op. 36, No. 4

Im Volkston

O Son - nen - schein! o Son - nen - schein! Wie___
O shin - ing sun, O shin - ing sun! How___

scheinst du mir in's Herz hin - ein, weck'st drin - nen lau - ter
you do shine in - to my heart, you wak - en there pure

Lie - bes - lust, dass___ mir so en - ge wird die Brust!
thoughts of love, That___ all too nar - row grows my breast!

VII₇
of V

26. Brahms (1833—1897), *Wiegenlied,* Op. 49, No. 4

will,   wirst du   wie - der   ge - weckt,   mor - gen
rest,   *May thy*   *slum - ber*   *be*   *blest,*   *Lay thee*

V₇
of IV

früh,   wenn Gott will,   wirst du   wie - der   ge - weckt.
down   *now and rest,*   *May thy*   *slum - ber*   *be*   *blest.*

15

4

The Cadential I$^6_4$ Chord

27. Mozart (1756—1791), *The Marriage of Figaro,* Act I, No. 9

16

po - so, Nar - ci - set - to, A - don - ci - no d'a - mor, - mor.

qui - et, sweet Nar - cis - sus, A - don - is of love, love.

28. Verdi (1813–1901), *Il Trovatore,* Act III, No. 18

Ah sì, ben mio; col - l'es - - se - re io

Ah yes, my love; to be with you as

tuo, tu mia con - sor - te,

yours, who are my plight - ed,

29. Mozart (1756–1791), *Variations on a theme by Duport,* K. 573

Tempo primo (adagio)

30. Schubert (1797–1828), *Der Wanderer,* Op. 4, No. 1

Wo   bist   du,   wo   bist   du,   mein   ge - lieb   - tes
Where   art   thou,   where   art   thou,   my   be - lov   - ed

Land? ge - sucht_____ ge - ahnt,_____ und
land? I've sought thee in vain_____ and

nie_____ ge - kannt!
known_____ thee not!

5

The II and II₆ Chords

31. Mozart (1756–1791), *Symphony in D Major,* K. 385

32. Mozart (1756–1791), *Divertimento,* No. 16, K. 289

33. Verdi (1813—1901), *Rigoletto,* Act I, No. 9

Ca - ro no - me che il mio cor fe - sti
Ah sweet name that made my heart first to

pri - mo pal - pi - tar, le de - li - zie del - l'a -
beat with lov - ing joy, Ah de - lights of that sweet

mor mi dêi sem - pre ram - men - tar!
love I shall al - ways hold them dear!

34. Schubert (1797—1828), *Waltz,* Op. 9a, No. 3

35. Mozart (1756–1791), *The Magic Flute,* Act I, No. 8

36. Verdi (1813–1901), *Nabucco,* Act IV, "Marcia funebre"

Allegro moderato assai

37. Chopin (1810–1849), *Waltz in G–flat Major,* Op. 70, No. 1

Meno mosso (♩ = 96)

cantabile
p

38. Bellini (1801–1835), *Norma,* Act II, No. 9

Deh! con te, con te li pren - di; li sos - tie - ni, li di
Take them with you, take them with you; keep them safe, from harm de -

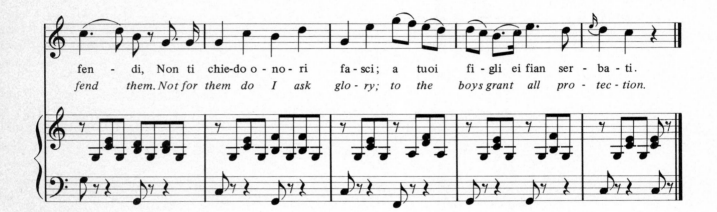

fen - di, Non ti chie-do o - no - ri fa - sci; a tuoi fi - gli ei fian ser - ba - ti.
fend them. Not for them do I ask glo - ry; to the boys grant all pro - tec - tion.

6

The I₆, IV₆, and V₆ Chords

39. J.S. Bach (1685—1750), *Was Gott Tut*

What - e'er my God or - dains is right; Where - fore I trust Him sure - ly.

40. Schubert (1797—1828), *Sonatina for Violin and Piano,* Op. 137, No. 3

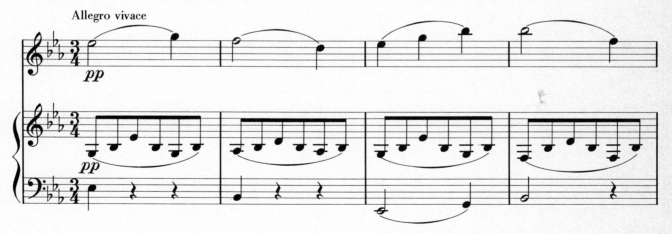

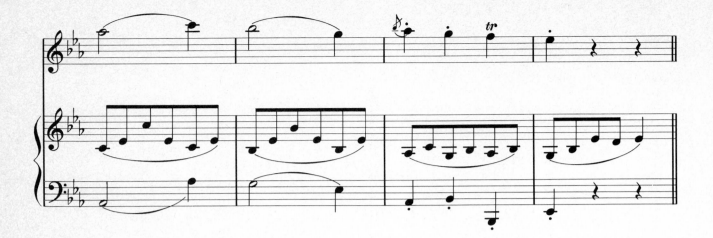

41. Haydn (1732—1809), *String Quartet,** Op. 3, No. 5

* The viola is tacet during this passage.

26

42. Haydn (1732—1809), *Capriccio*

43. Handel (1685—1759), *Messiah,* No. 4

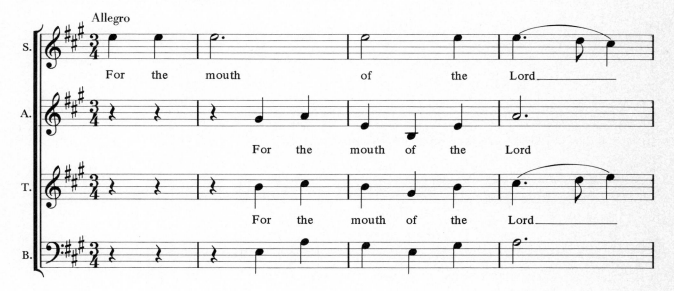

S. For the mouth of the Lord____

A. For the mouth of the Lord

T. For the mouth of the Lord____

B.

44. D. Scarlatti (1685—1757), *Toccata in D Minor*, L. 422

45. Corelli (1653–1713), *Concerto Grosso,* Op. 6, No. 8

46. J.S. Bach (1685–1750), *Vater unser im Himmelreich*

Our Fa - ther Thou in heav'n a - bove,

47. Saint-Saëns (1835–1921), *Sonata for Clarinet with Piano Accompaniment,* Op. 167

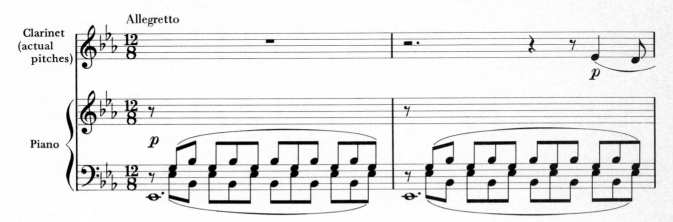

48. J.S. Bach (1685–1750), *Partita VI in E Minor*

7

The Inversions of the V₇ Chord

49. Brahms (1833–1897), *Trio II,** Op. 40

* The violin is tacet during this passage.

50. Mozart (1756–1791), *Piano Sonata in G Major,* K. 283

51. Bruch (1838–1920), *Kol Nidrei,* for Cello and Orchestra, Op. 47

52. Haydn (1732–1809), *Piano Sonata in C Major,* No. 5

53. Beethoven (1770–1827), *Piano Sonata,* Op. 31, No. 3

54. Mozart (1756–1791), *String Quintet in G Minor,* K. 516

II 2

55. Beethoven (1770–1827), *Piano Sonata,* Op. 57

56. Schubert (1797—1828), *Die schöne Müllerin,* Op. 25, No. 16

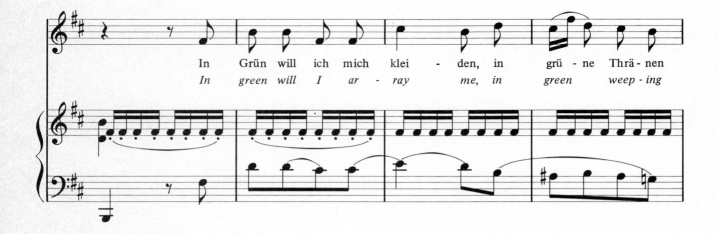

In Grün will ich mich klei - den, in grü - ne Thrä - nen
In green will I ar - ray me, in green weep - ing

wei - den! Mein Schatz hat's Grün so gern, mein Schatz hat's Grün so gern.
wil - low! My loved one's fond of green, My loved one's fond of green.

57. Beethoven (1770—1827), *Rondo,* Op. 51, No. 1

Moderato e grazioso

58. Beethoven (1770–1827), *String Quartet,* Op. 18, No. 6

Adagio, ma non troppo

II^6_5

36

8

Six-Four Chords

SECTION A: EMBELLISHING

59. Schumann (1810—1856), *Album for the Young,* Op. 68, No. 8

60. D. Scarlatti (1685—1757), *Sonata in C Major,* L. 457

61. Schumann (1810—1856), *Piano Sonata,* Op. 11

62. Verdi (1813—1901), *La Traviata,* Act I, No. 6

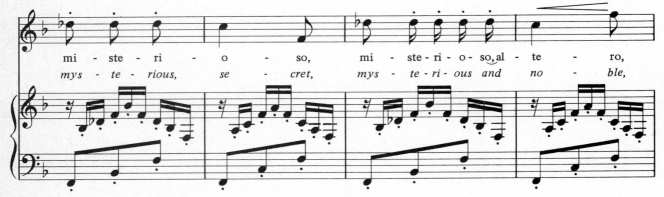

63. Mozart (1756–1791), *Piano Sonata in C Major,* K. 545

Andante

p dolce

legato

Embellishing
diminished 7th Chord

VI

legato

f

dim.

64. Beethoven (1770—1827), *Piano Sonata,* Op. 2, No. 3

65. Beethoven (1770—1827), *Piano Sonata,* Op. 2, No. 1

66. Mozart (1756—1791), *Symphony in G Minor,* K. 550

67. Haydn (1732—1809), *The Creation*, No. 14

Allegro

S. The heav-ens are tell-ing the glo-ry of God,_____ (acc.)

A. The heav-ens are tell-ing the glo-ry of God, (acc.)

T. The heav-ens are tell-ing the glo-ry of God,_____ (acc.)

B. The heav-ens are tell-ing the glo-ry of God, (acc.)

The_ won-der of His work dis-plays the fir-ma-ment.

The won-der of His work dis-plays the fir-ma-ment.

The won-der of His work dis-plays the fir-ma-ment.

The won-der of His work dis-plays the fir-ma-ment.

II$_5^6$

68. Rameau (1683—1764), *The Temple of Glory*

Gai

SECTION C: OTHER USES

69. Schubert (1797–1828), *Ländler,* Op. 67, No. 16

70. Mozart (1756–1791), *Symphony in E-flat Major,* K. 543

71. Beethoven (1770–1827), *Piano Sonata,* Op. 7

72. Beethoven (1770–1827), *Piano Sonata,* Op. 49, No. 2

73. Mozart (1756–1791), *Piano Concerto in B-flat Major,* K. 595

74. Beethoven (1770–1827), *Piano Sonata,* Op. 2, No. 1

75. Haydn (1732—1809), *Piano Sonata in C Major*, No. 5

VI

9

The VI and VI₆ Chords

76. J.S. Bach (1685—1750), *In Dich hab' ich gehoffet, Herr*

In Thee, Lord, have_____ I put my trust; Now and when life is end - - ing.

have I put_____ my

77. Mozart (1756—1791), *Quintet in A Major,* K. 581

78. Mendelssohn (1809—1847), *Sonata for Cello and Piano,* Op. 45

79. Schubert (1797—1828), *Winterreise,* **Op. 89, No. 11**

Etwas bewegt

Ich träum - te von bun - ten Blu - men, so wie sie wohl blü - hen im
I dreamt of col - ored flow - ers, The kind that blos - som in

Mai; ich träum - te von grü - nen Wie - sen, von lu - sti-gem Vo - gel-ge -
May; I dreamt of the green mead - ows, And mer - ry songs of the

schrei, von lu - sti-gem Vo - gel-ge - schrei.
birds, And mer - ry songs of the birds.

80. Mozart (1756—1791), *Symphony in C Major,* **K. 425**

Menuetto

81. Wagner (1813—1883), *Parsifal,* Act I

82. Beethoven (1770—1827), *Sonata for Violin and Piano,* Op. 24

83. Dvořák (1841–1904), *Symphony IX,* Op. 95

84. Wagner (1813–1883), *Lohengrin,* Prelude

85. J.S. Bach (1685–1750), *O Gott, du frommer Gott*

The work I thus have wrought, For Thou must give suc - cess.

86. Haydn (1732–1809), *Piano Sonata in C Major,* No. 16

87. Mozart (1756–1791), *The Magic Flute,* Act II, No. 18

88. Buxtehude (1637–1707), *Prelude and Fugue for Organ*

Manuals

Pedal

Motive

89. Brahms (1833–1897), *Symphony III,* Op. 90

Andante

p

più p

poco rit.

8va

90. Schubert (1797—1828), *Du bist die Ruh'*, Op. 59, No. 3

Du bist die Ruh', der Frie - de mild,
Thou art my rest, my sooth - ing peace,

die Sehn - sucht du, und was sie stillt;
As - suage my woes, and make them cease;

10

The III and III₆ Chords

91. Bourgeois (c. 1510—c. 1561), *Doxology* ("Old Hundredth")

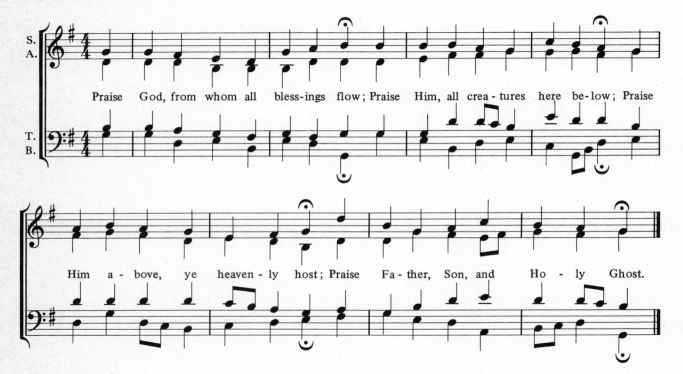

Praise God, from whom all bless-ings flow; Praise Him, all crea - tures here be - low; Praise

Him a - bove, ye heaven - ly host; Praise Fa - ther, Son, and Ho - ly Ghost.

92. Brahms (1833—1897), *Symphony IV*, Op. 98

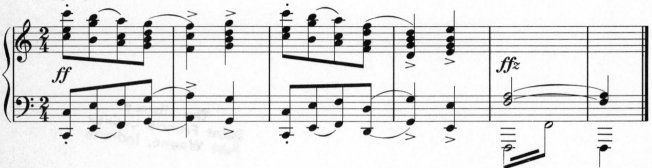

Allegro giocoso

52

93. Dvořák (1841–1904), *Symphony IX,* **Op. 95**

VI₇

94. Mozart (1756–1791), *The Marriage of Figaro,* **Act II, No. 10**

Por - gi a - mor,_____ qual - che ri - sto - ro
Grant, *O* *love,_____* *some* *con - so - la - tion*

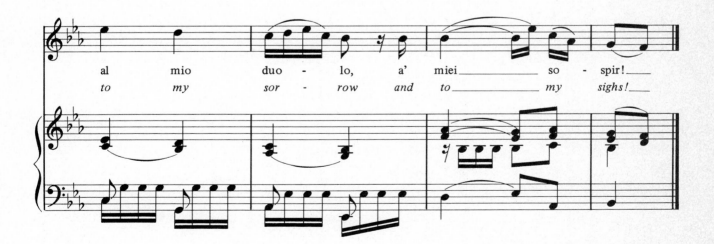

al mio duo - lo, a' miei_____ so - spir!_____
to *my* *sor - row* *and* *to_____* *my* *sighs!_____*

95. Mozart (1756—1791), *Requiem Mass,* K. 626, No. 8

Do - mi - ne Je - su Chri - ste, rex glo - ri - ae, rex glo - ri - ae!
Lord, Sav - iour Je - sus Christ,_____ O glo - rious king, O glo - rious king!

Do - mi - ne Je - su Chri - ste, rex glo - ri - ae, rex glo - ri - ae!
Lord, Sav - iour Je - sus Christ,_____ O glo - rious king, O glo - rious king!

Do - mi - ne Je - su Chri - ste, rex glo - ri - ae, rex glo - ri - ae!
Lord, Sav - iour Je - sus Christ,_____ O glo - rious king, O glo - rious king!

Do - mi - ne, Je - su Chri - ste, rex glo - ri - ae, rex glo - ri - ae!
Lord, Sav - iour Je - sus Christ,_____ O glo - rious king, O glo - rious king!

96. Dvořák (1841—1904), *Symphony IX,* Op. 95

97. Tchaikovsky (1840—1893), *Symphony IV*, Op. 36

98. Tchaikovsky (1840—1893), *Symphony IV*, Op. 36

99. Verdi (1813—1901), *Otello,* Act IV

100. Moussorgsky (1839—1881), *Boris Godunov*

101. Rameau (1683—1764), *The Temple of Glory*

11

The VII and VII₆ Chords

102. Schumann (1810—1856), *Album for the Young,* Op. 68, No. 4

103. Handel (1685—1759), *Messiah,* No. 2

104. Caldara (1670–1736), *Alma del Core*

Al - ma del co - re, spir - to dell' al - ma,
Soul of my heart, Spir - it of my soul

sem - pre co - stan - te t'a - do - re - rò.
al - ways faith - ful - ly you I'll a - dore.

105. Mozart (1756–1791), *Piano Sonata in B-flat Major,* K. 281

106. Schumann (1810—1856), *Album for the Young,* Op. 68, No. 9

107. J.S. Bach (1685—1750), *Little Preludes and Fugues for Organ*

Manuals

Pedal

108. Handel (1685—1759), *Organ Concerto in F Major,* No. 13

Manuals

Pedal

109. Haydn (1732—1809), *Piano Sonata in F Major,* No. 14

VII_2^4 VII_3^4

110. Sibelius (1865–1957), *Finlandia,* Op. 26

VII₆
of II

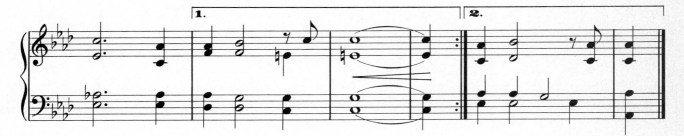

61

12

Successive First Inversions

111. Gluck (1714—1787), *Alceste,* Act III, No. 4

Leb' ein - ge - denk __ der Zärt - lich - keit __ ei - ner Gat - tin, die dir nur

Live __ to keep __ the sweet re - mem -brance of a wife __ who was e - ver

leb - te, die nur nach dei - ner Lie - be streb -

dear to you, who on - ly lived that she might please __

-te,   und sich für dich dem To - de weiht.

you,   and who for you would e - ven die.

112. Handel (1685–1759), *Messiah,* No. 29

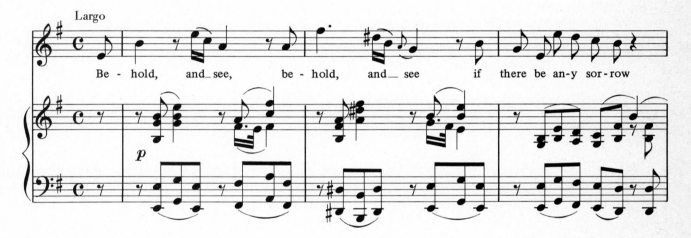

Be - hold,   and_ see,   be - hold,   and_ see   if there be an-y sor - row

like un - to His sor - row.

113. J.S. Bach (1685–1750), *Suite in G Minor for Clavier*

* In some editions, this note appears as G.

114. Haydn (1732–1809), *Symphony in D Major*, No. 104

115. Handel (1685–1759), *Sonata in A Minor,* Op. 1, No. 4

* *Flauto* as used in Handel's day meant "recorder."

116. Mozart (1756–1791), *Piano Sonata in C Major,* K. 279

13

Sequence

117. Schubert (1797—1828), *Symphony VII*

118. Beethoven (1770—1827), *Piano Sonata*, Op. 109

119. J.S. Bach (1685—1750), *Well-Tempered Clavier*, Book I, Prelude 21

120. Haydn (1732—1809), *Piano Sonata in D Major,* No. 9

121. Corelli (1653—1713), *Violin Sonata,* Op. 5, No. 9

II$^6_5$

122. Mozart (1756—1791), *Piano Sonata in C Major*, K. 545

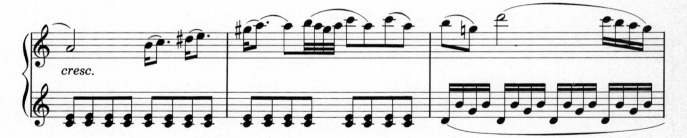

123. Handel (1685—1759), *Suite VII*, Passacaglia

Allegro comodo

124. Chopin (1810—1849), *Étude,* Op. 25, No. 9

Allegro assai

$$V_5^6$$
of V

$$V_5^6$$
of V

14

The II₇ Chord and Its Inversions

125. J.S. Bach (1685–1750), *Ach Gott, erhör' mein Seufzen*

O hear, my God, my pray'r and sore com - plain - - ing.

126. J.S. Bach (1685–1750), *Meine Augen schliess' ich jetzt*

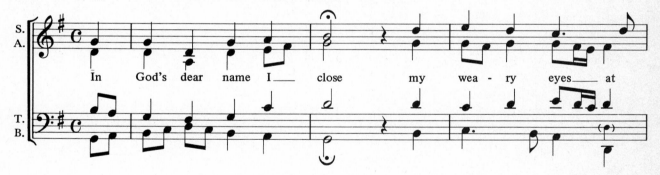

In God's dear name I__ close my wea - ry eyes__ at

last when comes__ the dark__ of mid - - night.

127. Handel (1685–1759), *Messiah,* No. 43

I know that___ my Re - deem - er liv - eth.

128. Handel (1685–1759), *Rinaldo,* Act II, No. 31

La - scia   ch'io pian - ga   mia cru - da sor - te
Let me   la - ment then   my cru - el for - tune

e che so___ spi - ri   la li - ber - tà.
and that I should   sigh for   my li - ber - ty.

129. Chopin (1810—1849), *Waltz,* Op. 69, No. 2

130. Wolf (1860—1903), *Wiegenlied*

Su, su, su ihr Eng - lein, küsst ihm leis die Wäng - lein
Su, su, su dear an - gels, kiss his soft cheeks gen - tly

dass es lie - ge in der Wie - ge wie in Pa - ra - die - ses Schoss!
that he may lie in the cra - dle as in lap of par - a - dise.

Schlaf!   Schlaf!   Schlaf!   Schlaf!
Sleep!   *Sleep!*   *Sleep!*   *Sleep!*

131. J. Strauss (1825—1899), *Tales from the Vienna Woods,* Op. 325

132. Schubert (1797–1828), *Serenade*

Lei - se fle - hen   mei - ne Lie - der   durch   die Nacht zu   dir;
Light - ly float - ing   *come— my songs—*   *through   the night   to   you;*

133. Tchaikovsky (1840–1893), *Symphony V*, Op. 64

134. Pergolesi (1710–1736), *Se tu m'ami*

Se tu__ m'a - mi,__ se tu so - spi - ri Sol__ per
If you__ love me,__ if you sigh on - ly But__ for

me,_ gen - til pa__ stor,____
me,_ O gen - tle__ swain,____

135. Randall Thompson (1899—), *Alleluia*

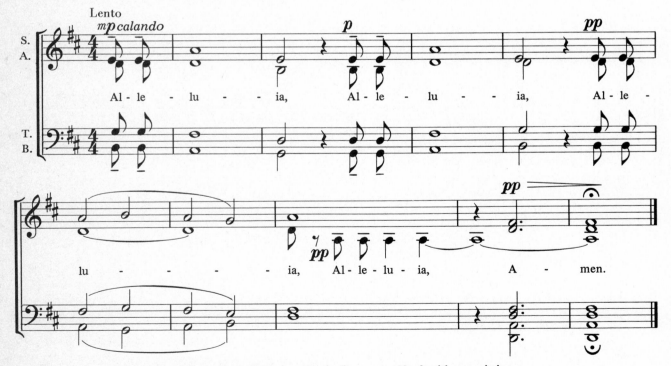

Al - le - lu - ia, Al - le - lu - ia, Al - le -

lu - - - - ia, Al - le - lu - ia, A - men.

136. Mozart (1756—1791), *Symphony in G Minor,* K. 550

137. Beethoven (1770—1827), *Piano Sonata,* Op. 14, No. 2

138. J.S. Bach (1685—1750), *Partita II for Unaccompanied Violin,* Chaconne

15

The VII₇ Chord and Its Inversions

139. Mozart (1756—1791), *Sonata in G Major for Violin and Piano*, K. 379

78

140. Beethoven (1770—1827), *Piano Sonata,* Op. 10, No. 1

141. Beethoven (1770—1827), *Symphony III*, Op. 55

142. J.S. Bach (1685—1750), *Passacaglia in C Minor*, for organ

143. Haydn (1732–1809), *String Quartet,* Op. 17, No. 5

144. Dvořák (1841–1904), *String Quartet,* Op. 96

(Piano Reduction)

145. Bruch (1838—1920), *Violin Concerto in G Minor,* Op. 26

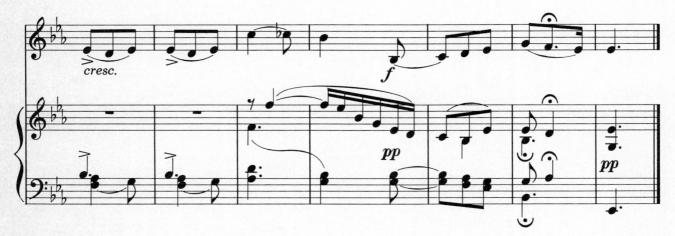

146. Gluck (1714—1787), *Orfeo,* Act I, No. 1

147. Brahms (1833—1897), *Ballade,* Op. 10, No. 4

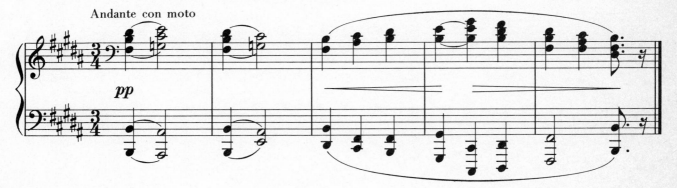

16

Other Seventh Chords

148. J.S. Bach (1685–1750), *Werde munter, mein Gemüte*

Hear my ear - nest prayer, O hear me! Lord, Thou hear - est, Thou art near me.

149. J.S. Bach (1685–1750), *Saint Matthew Passion,* No. 16

The sor - rows Thou art bear - ing, 'Tis I that should en - dure it all.

150. J.S. Bach (1685–1750), *Jesus selbst, mein Licht, mein Leben*

Je - sus Christ, my Pride, my Glo - ry, He, the true and liv - ing Light.

151. Kuhlau (1786–1832), *Piano Sonatina,* Op. 88, No. 3

152. Mozart (1756–1791), *Piano Sonata in F Major,* K. 533

153. J.S. Bach (1685–1750), *Christmas Oratorio,* No. 41

154. Corelli (1653–1713), *Sonata,* Op. 5, No. 1

155. Vivaldi (c. 1678–1741), J.S. Bach (1685–1750), *Organ Concerto in D Minor*

156. Byrd (1538—1623), *Pavan,* The Earl of Salisbury

157. Puccini (1858—1924), *La Rondine,* Act I

158. Bizet (1838–1875), *Carmen,* Act II, No. 17

La fleur que tu m'a- vais je - tè - e, Dans ma pri - son___ m'é - tait res - té - e, Flé -
This flow - er that you tossed to me,___ In pris - on I___ have kept with me,___ Though

trie et sè - che, cet - te fleur Gar - dait tou - jours___ sa douce o - deur;
dead and dry___ it now may be, It keeps al - ways___ its sweet per - fume.

Embellishing
diminished 7th

159. Puccini (1858—1924), *La Bohème,* Act IV

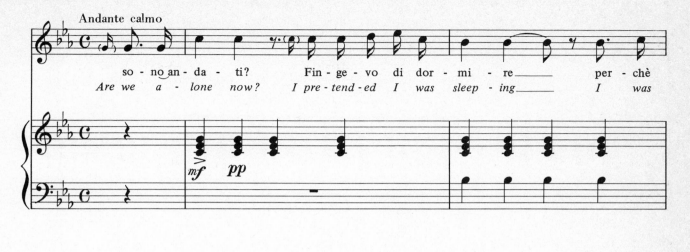

160. Schumann (1810—1856), *Dichterliebe,* Op. 48, No. 7

Ich grol - le nicht, und wenn das Herz_____ auch bricht,
I'll not com - plain al - though my heart_____ should break,

e - wig ver - lor' - nes Lieb, e - wig ver - lor' - nes Lieb!_____ ich
Love ev - er lost to me, Love ev - er lost to me!_____ I'll

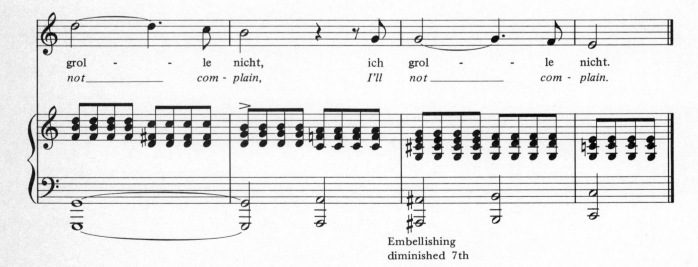

grol - - le nicht, ich grol - - le nicht.
not_____ com - plain, I'll not_____ com - plain.

Embellishing
diminished 7th

161. Samuel Barber (1910—), *String Quartet,* Op. 11

Copyright 1943, 1971 by G. Schirmer, Inc. Used by permission.

17

Secondary Dominants

SECTION A: OF V

162. Verdi (1813—1901), *Falstaff,* Act II, Scene I

C'è a Wind - sor u - na da - ma bel - la e leg - gia - dra mol - to.
In Wind - sor lives a la - dy love - ly and ver - y charm - ing.

163. Mozart (1756—1791), *Symphony in G Minor,* K. 550

164. Haydn (1732—1809), *String Quartet,* Op. 76, No. 5

165. Beethoven (1770—1827), *Piano Sonata,* Op. 7

Largo, con grand' espressione

166. Vitali (1665? —?), *Chaconne*

167. Fauré (1845—1924), *Quartet in C Minor,* Op. 15

168. Mozart (1756—1791), *Mass in C Major,* K. 317

169. Beethoven (1770—1827), *Piano Sonata,* Op. 110

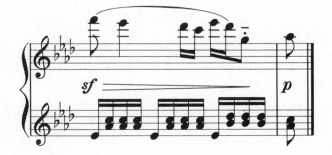

170. Beethoven (1770–1827), *Piano Sonata,* Op. 10, No. 3

171. Schubert (1797–1828), *Symphony V*

172. Schubert (1797—1828), *Symphony VIII*

173. R. Strauss (1864—1949), *Serenade*, Op. 7

174. Beethoven (1770—1827), *Trio,* Op. 1, No. 2

175. Mozart (1756—1791), *Piano Sonata in D Major,* K. 311

176. Beethoven (1770–1827), *Andante Favori*

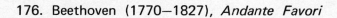

177. Mozart (1756–1791), *Piano Concerto in G Major*, K. 453

178. Beethoven (1770—1827), *String Quartet,* Op. 135

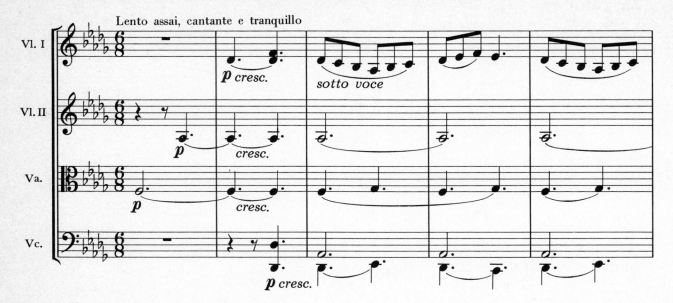

179. Dvořák (1841—1904), *Symphony VII,* Op. 70

180. Mendelssohn (1809—1847), *Songs Without Words,* Op. 19, No. 2

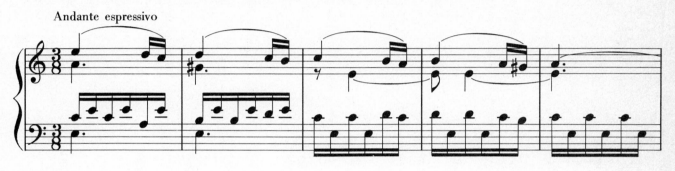

181. Mozart (1756—1791), *Symphony in G Minor,* K. 550

182. Verdi (1813—1901), *La Traviata,* Act I, No. 6

Ah, for - s'è lui che l'a - ni - ma
Ah, is it he my heart fore - saw

so - lin - ga ne' tu - mul - ti, so - lin - ga ne' tu - mul - ti.
lone - ly in the throng lone - ly in the throng.

183. Schubert (1797—1828), *Symphony VII*

184. Schubert (1797—1828), *Symphony VIII*

185. Tchaikovsky (1840—1893), *Ouverture-Fantaisie,* "Romeo et Juliette"

186. Tchaikovsky (1840—1893), *Ouverture-Fantaisie,* "Francesca da Rimini," Op. 32

187. Handel (1685—1759), *Messiah,* No. 37a

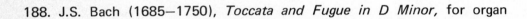

188. J.S. Bach (1685—1750), *Toccata and Fugue in D Minor,* for organ

18

Diminished Seventh Chords:
Dominant Function

SECTION A: OF V

189. Schumann (1810–1856), *Scenes from Childhood,* Op. 15, No. 1

190. Beethoven (1770–1827), *Piano Sonata,* Op. 10, No. 3

SECTION B: OF IV

191. Schumann (1810–1856), *Der arme Peter,* Op. 53, No. 3c

Der ar - me Pe - ter wankt vor - bei gar lang - sam, lei - chen - blass und scheu,
Now poor young Pe - ter tot - ters by, Quite slow - ly, pale as death, and shy:

192. Gluck (1714–1787), *Orfeo,* Act II, No. 18

193. Mozart (1756–1791), *Piano Sonata in F Major,* K. 547a

194. Schubert (1797–1828), *Ländler,* Op. 171, No. 2

SECTION D: OF VI

195. Mozart (1756–1791), *Piano Sonata in B-flat Major,* K. anh. 136

196. Beethoven (1770–1827), *String Quartet,* Op. 18, No. 2

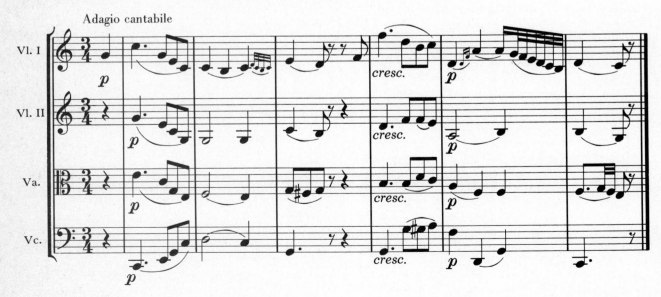

197. Sibelius (1865—1957), *Symphony I,* Op. 39

SECTION E: OF III

198. Brahms (1833—1897), *Waltzes,* Op. 39, No. 4

19

Diminished Seventh Chords:
Non-Dominant Function

199. Rossini (1792—1868), *Semiramide,* Overture

200. Mendelssohn (1809—1847), *Rondo Capriccioso,* Op. 14

201. Bizet (1838–1875), *L'Arlésienne Suite,* No. 1

202. Schubert (1797–1828), *Trio,* Op. 99

203. Schumann (1810—1856), *Variations on the Name "Abegg,"* Op. 1

112

20

Modulation to the
Dominant Key (Major Mode)

204. J.S. Bach (1685—1750), *Heilig, heilig, heilig*

no - mi - ne Do - mi - ni. O - - san - na in ex - cel - sis.
the name — of the Lord. Ho - - san - na in the high - est.

205. Haydn (1732—1809), *Symphony in C Major,* No. 97

206. Haydn (1732—1809), *Symphony in D Major,* No. 104

207. Tchaikovsky (1840—1893), *Variations sur un Thème rococo,* Op. 33

208. Tchaikovsky (1840—1893), *Symphony V,* Op. 64

209. Weber (1786–1826), *Der Freischütz,* Act II, No. 9

Lei - se, lei - se, from - me Wei - se, schwing' dich auf zum Ster-nen -
Soft - ly, soft - ly, gen - tle mus - sic Soar - ing up - ward to the

krei - se! Lied, er - schal - le, fei - ernd wal - le
stars - a - bove! Song, ring out in fes - tive man - ner,

mein Ge - bet zur Him - mels - hal - le!
With my prayer to heav - en's hall!

210. Schubert (1797–1828), *Heidenröslein,* Op. 3, No. 3

118

211. Mozart (1756–1791), *Piano Sonata,* K. 284

212. Beethoven (1770—1827), *Piano Sonata,* Op. 14, No. 2

21

Modulation to the
Dominant Key (Minor Mode)

213. J.S. Bach (1685–1750), *Was fürchst du, Feind Herodes, sehr*

The star pro - claims the King _____ is here;

But, Her - od why this sense - less fear?

214. Beethoven (1770–1827), *Piano Sonata*, Op. 10, No. 3

Presto

215. Schumann (1810—1856), *Symphony IV,* Op. 120

216. Mozart (1756—1791), *Symphony in G Minor,* K. 550

217. Mozart (1756—1791), *Serenade for Eight Winds*, K. 388

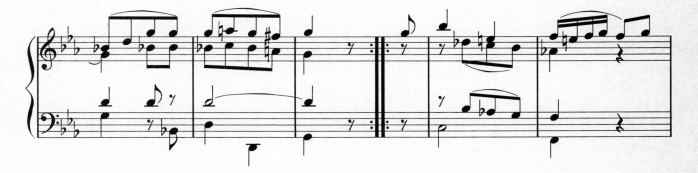

218. Mozart (1756–1791), *Serenade for Thirteen Winds,* K. 361

22

Modulation from the Minor
to the Relative Major Key

219. J.S. Bach (1685—1750), *Saint John Passion*, No. 4

O won - drous Love, whose depths no heart has sound - ed, That brought Thee here by sin and grief sur - round - ed, We live, the plea - sures of this world en - joy - ing; And Thou art dy - ing.

220. Schubert (1797–1828), *Der Wanderer,* Op. 4, No. 1

Die Son - ne dünkt mich hier so kalt, die Blü - the welk, das Le - ben alt, und
The sun to me seems dim and cold, The flow'rs are pale, and life seems old;

was sie re - den, lee - rer Schall, ich bin ein Fremd - ling ü - ber - all.
Their speech does seem but emp - ty sound, And strang - er I on for - eign ground.

221. J.S. Bach (1685–1750), *English Suite III*

222. Haydn (1732—1809), *Trio II in F-sharp Minor*

223. Schumann (1810–1856), *Symphonic Études,* Op. 13

224. Purcell (1658–1695), *Dido and Aeneas,* Act I, No. 4

When mon - archs u - nite, how hap - py their

state, They tri-umph at once o'er their foes and their fate, they

state, They tri-umph at once o'er their foes and their fate, they

state, They tri-umph at once o'er their foes and their fate, they

state, They tri-umph at once o'er their foes and their fate, they

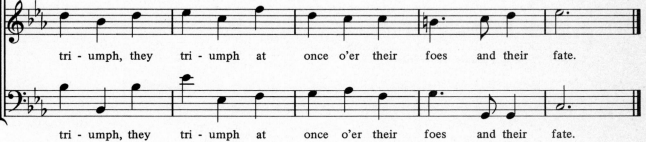

tri-umph, they tri-umph at once o'er their foes and their fate.

tri-umph, they tri-umph at once o'er their foes and their fate.

tri-umph, they tri-umph at once o'er their foes and their fate.

tri-umph, they tri-umph at once o'er their foes and their fate.

225. J.S. Bach (1685–1750), *Little Notebook for Anna Magdalena Bach*

23

Modulation to Other
Closely Related Keys

226. J.S. Bach (1658–1750), *Nun preiset alle Gottes Barmherzigkeit*

227. J.S. Bach (1685–1750), *O Haupt voll Blut und Wunden*

O sa-cred Head, now wound-ed, With grief and shame weighed down, Now

scorn-ful-ly sur-round-ed, With thorns, Thine on-ly crown. Mine

eyes shall then be-hold___ Thee, Up-on Thy cross shall dwell, My

heart by faith en-fold___ Thee. Who di-eth thus, dies well.

228. J.S. Bach (1685—1750), *Jesu, der du meine Seele*

1. Je - sus, by Thy Cross and Pas - sion, By the bit - ter pain Thou bore,
2. When the E - vil One would hold me, Deep in__ Hell to__ suf - fer sore,

Might - i - ly a - way Thou bore me, With a__ ha - ven safe be - fore me,

Through Thy Word, con - tent - ment sweet, Thou art still my sure re - treat.

133

229. J.S. Bach (1685–1750), *Herzlich lieb hab' ich dich, O Herr*

Lord, Thee I love with all my heart; I pray Thee, ne'er from

me de - part, With ten - der mer - cy cheer_____me.

230. J.S. Bach (1685–1750), *French Suite II*

231. Beethoven (1770–1827), *String Quartet,* Op. 59, No. 2

232. Chopin (1810–1849), *Mazurka,* Op. 59, No. 2

233. Franz (1815–1892), *Marie,* Op. 18

Marie, am Fen - ster si - tzest du, du lie - bes, sü - sses Kind,___ und
Ma - rie, you sit at win-dow there, you dear, sweet, gen - tle child,___ You

siehst dem Spiel der Blü - ten zu, ver - weht im A - - bend-wind.___
see the play of blos-soms there, Toss'd by the eve - - ning air.___

234. Lvov (1798–1870), *Russian Hymn*

God ev - er glo - ri - ous, Sov - 'reign of all, Vouch - safe Thy

God ev - er glo - ri - ous, Sov - 'reign of all, Vouch - safe Thy

136

bless - ing on our own dear land. Thine is the vic - to - ry, and

bless - ing on our own dear land. Thine is the vic - to - ry, and

Thine the king - ly pow'r Sent forth to de - liv - er by Thy might - y hand.

Thine the king - ly pow'r Sent forth to de - liv - er by Thy might - y hand.

235. Haydn (1732—1809), *String Quartet,* Op. 74, No. 3

236. Brahms (1833–1897), *Violin Concerto in D Major*, Op. 77

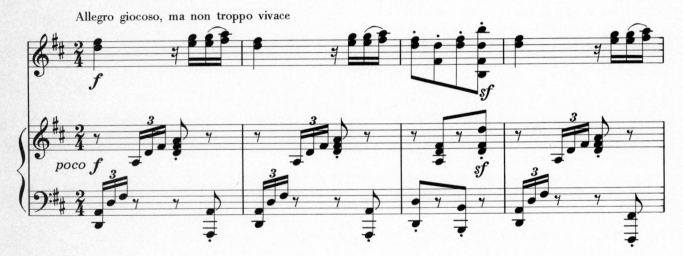

237. Schumann (1810–1856), *Dichterliebe,* Op. 48, No. 4

Wenn ich in dei - ne Au - gen seh', so
When I in - to your eyes look deep, *then*

schwin - det all' mein Leid und Weh'; doch wenn ich küs - se dei - nen
gone are all my grief and pain; *so when my lips your dear ones*

Mund, so werd' ich ganz und gar ge - sund.
press, my health re - vives from your ca - ress.

238. Handel (1685—1759), *Semele,* Act II, No. 36

Where - 'er you tread, the blush - ing flow'rs shall rise, and

all things flour - ish, and all things flour - ish where-

'er you turn your eyes, where -'er you turn your eyes, where-'er you turn your eyes.

24

The Neapolitan Chord

239. Beethoven (1770–1827), *Piano Sonata,* Op. 27, No. 2

240. Chopin (1810–1849), *Nocturne,* Op. 55, No. 1

241. Vivaldi (c. 1678–1741), J.S. Bach (1685–1750), *Organ Concerto in D Minor*

242. Schubert (1797–1828), *Sonatina for Violin and Piano*, Op. 137, No. 2

243. Beethoven (1770—1827), *Variations on "God Save the King"*

Con espressione

244. Schubert (1797–1828), *Die schöne Müllerin,* Op. 25, No. 19

Wo ein treu-es Her-ze in Lie-be ver geht, da
When a faith-ful heart doth for love___ pine a - way, Then

wel-ken die Li - lien auf je - dem Beet; da muss in die
all the___ li - lies___ fade,___ a - way; Then in - to the

Wol - ken der Voll - mond geh'n, da - mit sei - ne Thrä - nen die
clouds the___ full___ moon goes, so that her___ tears___ man -

Men - schen nicht seh'n;____ da hal - ten die Eng - lein die Au - gen sich
kind should not see;____ Then close the____ an - gels their eyes____ in____

zu und schluch -zen und sin - gen die See - le zur Ruh'.
sor - row, and sob and____ sing____ the soul____ to____ rest.

245. Schubert (1797—1828), *Winterreise,* Op. 89, No. 15

Etwas langsam
poco marc.

p

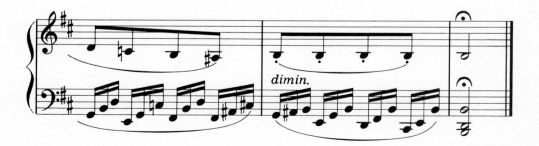

dimin.

246. Schubert (1797—1828), *Phantasie,* Op. 103

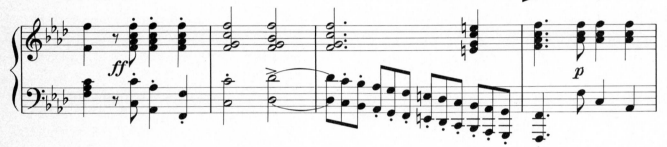

247. Schubert (1797—1828), *Nachtgesang*

Tie - fe Fei - er schau - ert um die Welt.
Deep so - lem - ni - ty des - cends up - on the earth!

Brau - ne Schlei - er hül - len Wald und Feld.
Brown___ haze en - vel - ops wood and field.

248. Haydn (1732—1809), *String Quartet,* Op. 76, No. 6

25

Augmented Sixth Chords

SECTION A: THE AUGMENTED SIXTH (ITALIAN)

249. Tartini (1692–1770), *Violin Sonata in G Minor, "The Devil's Trill"*

250. Beethoven (1770—1827), *String Quartet,* Op. 18, No. 2

251. Beethoven (1770—1827), *Bagatelle,* Op. 119, No. 1

252. Beethoven (1770—1827), *Sechs geistliche Lieder,* Op. 48, No. 4

Die Him - mel rüh - men des E - wi - gen
The heav'ns re - sound with His prais - es e -

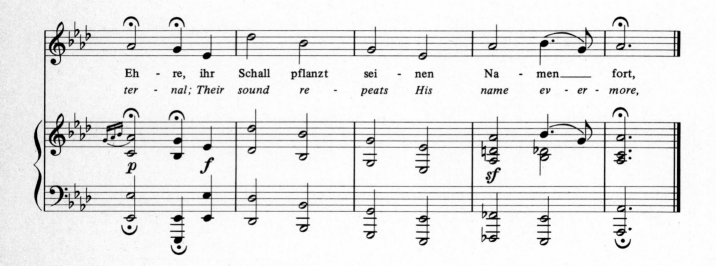

Eh - re, ihr Schall pflanzt sei - nen Na - men____ fort,
ter - nal; Their sound re - peats His name ev - er - more,

SECTION B: THE AUGMENTED
SIX-FIVE-THREE (GERMAN)

253. Beethoven (1770—1827), *Trio,* Op. 1, No. 3

254. Schumann (1810–1856), *Waltz,* Op. 124, No. 4

255. Brahms (1833–1897), *Symphony I,* Op. 68

256. Gluck (1714–1787), *Orfeo,* Act II, No. 30

257. Schubert (1797–1828), *Der Entfernten*

* Note that the two tenor voices are sung or played an octave lower than written.

154

258. Elgar (1857—1934), *Variations on an Original Theme* ("Enigma"), Op. 36

SECTION C: THE AUGMENTED
SIX-FOUR-THREE (FRENCH)

259. Schubert (1797—1828), *Gesänge des Harfners I*, Op. 12, No. 1

Ein - sam - keit er - gibt, ach! der ist bald al - lein;
yields to sol - i - tude, oh! he is soon a - lone.

260. Mozart (1756–1791), *String Quartet in C Major,* K. 465

261. Mozart (1756—1791), *Symphony in G Minor*, K. 550

262. Mozart (1756–1791), *Piano Sonata in D Major*, K. 284

263. Beethoven (1770—1827), *Trio,* **Op. 97**

Andante cantabile, ma però con moto
semplice

Reprinted from Peters Edition, No. 166A (II), *The 11 Celebrated Trios, Volume II,* by permission of the publisher, C. F. Peters Corporation, 373 Park Avenue South, New York 16, N.Y.

264. Schubert (1797—1828), *Hark, hark! the Lark*

Allegretto

Fine

Horch, horch, die Lerch' im Ä - ther - blau! und Phö - bus, neu_____ er -
Hark, hark! the lark at Heav'n's gate sings, And Phoe - bus, 'gins_____ to

weckt,_____ tränkt sei - ne Ro - sse mit dem Thau, der
rise,_____ His steeds to wa - ter at those springs, On

Blu - men - kel - che deckt,_____ der Blu - men - kel - che
chal - ic'd flow'rs that lies,_____ On chal - ic'd flow'rs that

deckt. Der Ring - el - blu - me Knos - pe schleusst_____ die
lies! And wink - ing Ma - ry - buds be - gin_____ To

gold - 'nen Äug - lein auf, mit al - lem, was___ da
ope their gold - en eyes, With ev - 'ry -thing___ that

rei - zend ist___ du sü - sse Maid,___ steh' auf, mit
pret - ty is, My La - dy sweet,___ a - rise, With

al - lem was___ da rei - zend ist___ du sü - sse Maid,___ steh'
ev - 'ry -thing___ that pret - ty is, My La - dy sweet,___ a -

cresc.

cresc.

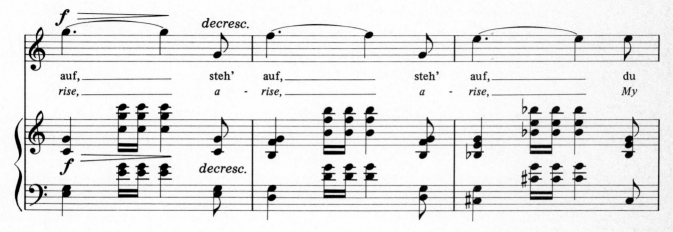

f

decresc.

auf,_____ steh' auf,_____ steh' auf,_____ du
rise,_____ a - rise,_____ a - rise,_____ My

f

decresc.

süße Maid, steh' auf, steh' auf, steh'
Lady sweet, a - rise, a - rise, a -

auf, du süße Maid, steh' auf!
rise, My Lady sweet, a - rise!

D.S. al Fine

265. Schubert (1797—1828), *Klärchens Lied*

Sehr langsam

Freud - voll und leid - voll, ge - dan - - ken - voll
Cheer - ful and tear - ful, and lost in

162

sein;   han - gen und ban - gen in
thought;   *yearn - ing and burn - ing in*

schwe - - ben-der Pein;   him - mel - hoch
pain - - ful sus - pense;   *ex - ult - ing to*

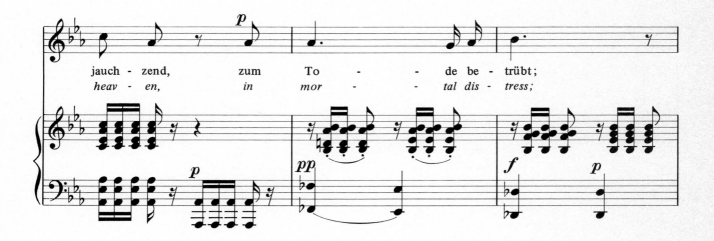

jauch - zend,   zum To - - de be - trübt;
heav - en,   *in mor - - tal dis - tress;*

glück - lich al - lein____ ist die See - le, die liebt, glück - lich al -
hap - py a - lone____ is the soul____ that loves, *hap - py a -*

lein_____ ist die See - le, die liebt.
lone_____ is the soul____ that loves.

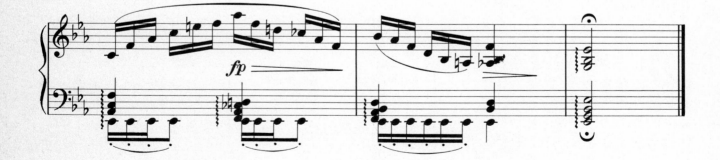

SECTION E: OTHER USES OF
THE AUGMENTED SIXTH CHORDS

266. Sibelius (1865—1957), *Finlandia*, Op. 26

267. Grieg (1843—1907), *The First Meeting*

268. Brahms (1833—1897), *Symphony I,* Op. 68

269. Schubert (1797—1828), *Symphony VIII*

26

The Whole-Tone Scale

Scales consisting entirely of whole steps can be constructed starting on C

and on C-sharp (D-flat)

Any attempt to construct a whole-tone scale on any other staff degree will result in a duplication of one of the above two, with various tones expressed enharmonically.

Any combination of the notes of the whole-tone scale may be used as a chord, including the entire six notes of the scale; but all of these chords have a similarity because of the presence of certain intervals and the absence of others. The only intervals that can be constructed from the whole-tone scale are the major second, major third, augmented fourth (diminished fifth), augmented fifth (minor sixth), augmented sixth (minor seventh), and perfect octave. The lack of a perfect fourth and perfect fifth makes the tonality vague, and the absence of a minor second and major seventh takes away "bite" or "pungency."

270. Debussy (1862—1918), *Préludes,* Book I, No. 2, "Voiles"

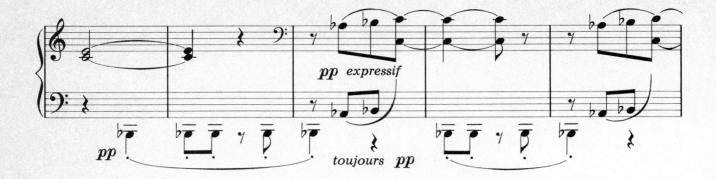

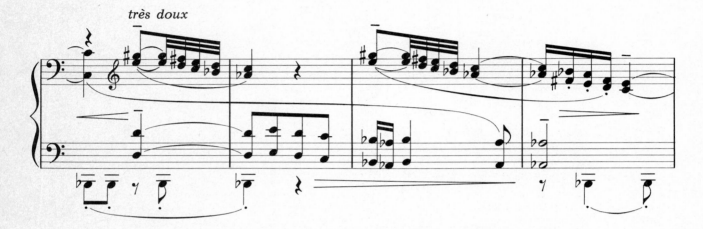

271. Puccini (1858–1924), *La Fanciulla del West,* Act I

272. Puccini (1858–1924), *Madama Butterfly,* Act II, First part

Ho cre - du - to mo - rir
I be - lieved I would die.
Ma pas - sa pre - sto co - me
But soon it pas - ses, just as

pas - san le nu - vo - le sul ma - re.
sha - dows that flit a - cross the o - cean.
Ah! m'ha scor - da - ta?
Ah! am I for - got - ten?

273. Puccini (1858–1924), *La Fanciulla del West,* Act I

In the following excerpt, observe that by the simultaneous use of the whole-tone scale built on both the C and C-sharp levels it is possible to obtain all the intervals available in the major-minor system.

274. Rochberg (1918—), *Psalm 23*

al may_____ me - nu - chot ye - na - ha - lay - nee._____
He lead - eth me_____ be - side still wa - ters._____

not de - she yar - bee - tsay - nee al may me - nu - chot ye -
me to lie down in green pas - tures: *He lead - eth me_____ be -*

de - she yar - bee - tsay - nee._____
to lie down in green pas - tures:_____

al may me - nu - chot ye - na - ha - lay - nee._____
He lead - eth me_____ be - side still wa - ters._____

na - ha - lay - nee._____
side still wa - ters._____

al may_____ me - nu - chot ye - na - ha - lay - nee._____
He lead - eth me_____ be - side still wa - ters._____

172

27

Quartal Harmony

Some twentieth-century compositions are composed either wholly or in part of chords built on fourths. By inversion and octave displacement these chords may appear to be built on fifths and seconds.

275. Ives (1874–1954), *Psalm XXIV*

right - eous - ness   from the   God   of his sal - va - tion.

right - eous - ness   from the   God   of his sal - va - tion.

right - eous - ness   from the   God   of his sal - va - tion.

right - eous - ness   from the   God   of his sal - va - tion.

In the following composition the notational errors of rhythm are left as in the original. Observe the scale construction of the vocal line in contrast to the chords of the piano accompaniment.

276. Ives (1874—1954), *The Cage*

Note: All notes not marked with sharp or flat are natural.
* If the "Middle C" were a C-sharp, this chord would be whole-tone harmony.

277. Bartók (1881–1945), *Fourteen Bagatelles,* Op. 6, No. 11

278. Ravel (1875–1937), *Ma Mère l'Oye,* "Laideronnette"

28

Polychords and Polytonality

Polychords (the simultaneous use of two or more different chords) may or may not imply polytonality. Polytonality (the simultaneous use of different tonalities in different parts or voices of a musical composition) can be purely chordal, purely contrapuntal, or a combination of chords and melodies in different keys.

279. Honegger (1892—1955), *Symphonie V*

280. William Schuman (1910—), *A Three-Score Set*

281. Milhaud (1892–), *Saudades do Brazil,* **No. 7, "Corcovado"**

282. Stravinsky (1882–1971), *Petroushka,* **Scene two**

283. Honegger (1892—1955), *Le Roi David,* "Third Fanfare"

284. Ives (1874–1954), *Variations on "America,"* First Interlude

29

Twelve-Tone Technique[1]

The right hand part of the following excerpt consists of three statements of the basic "set" (sometimes called "row" or "series"). Write out the set before beginning analysis.

285. Křenek (1900–), *Eight Piano Pieces,* No. 1, "Etude"

© 1946 by Mercury Music Corp. Reprinted by permission of Theodore Presser Company.

[1] For explanations of twelve-tone technique, see: Apel, *Harvard Dictionary of Music,* 2nd ed., article "Serial Music"; Dallin, *Techniques of Twentieth Century Composition,* chapter 14; Krenek, *Studies in Counterpoint;* Marquis, *Twentieth Century Music Idioms,* chapter 7; Perle, *Serial Composition and Atonality;* Schoenberg, *Style and Idea,* chapter 5; Ulehla, *Contemporary Harmony,* chapters 20 and 21.

The following excerpt is the beginning of the fourth of a group of twelve
pieces, all of which are based on

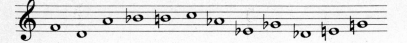

This quotation consists of a permutation of the original set.

286. Křenek (1900—), *Twelve Short Piano Pieces,* Op. 83, No. 4, "The Moon Rises"

In excerpt 287, the piano introduction *may* be considered as the original statement of the set. This excerpt can be analyzed on that basis.

However, since this is the beginning of the third of a cycle of three songs built on the same set, the original untransposed form of the set can be found only in reference to the beginning of Op. 23, No. 1:

287. Webern (1883–1945), *Drei Gesänge,* Op. 23, No. 3, "Herr Jesus mein"

In the next excerpt the basic set, found in the first violin, divides into four groups of three notes each. Segmentation of the set into four groups of three notes occurs throughout the three lower parts.

288. Schoenberg (1874–1951), *Fourth String Quartet,* Op. 37

The following song exemplifies Schoenberg's method of using his set in three segments of four notes each. The beginning of the vocal line states the set in its entirety.

In the piano introduction circle notes 1, 2, 3, 4 of the set; then notes 5, 6, 7, 8; and finally 9, 10, 11, 12. Similar treatment will clarify the set content of the rest of the song.

289. Schoenberg (1874–1951), *Three Songs,* Op. 48, No. 2, "Tot"

Was liegt da-ran! Ist al - les eins,
What mat - ters it! If all's the same,

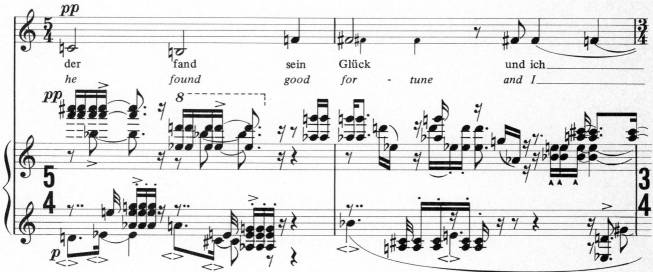

der fand sein Glück und ich_____
he found good for - tune and I_____

_____ fand keins.
_____ found none.

187

Supplementary Excerpts

1 The I Chord and Nonharmonic Tones

J. S. Bach, *Partita in E Major for Unaccompanied Violin*, "Preludio" (1-17)*
  Two-Part Invention No. 8 (1-5)
Beethoven, *Piano Concerto IV*, Op. 58, first movement (last 8)
  Piano Sonatas: Op. 2, No. 3, first movement (13-17); Op. 22, first movement (1-4)
  Symphony I, Op. 21, first movement (last 22)
  Symphony II, Op. 36, first movement (73-76)
  Trio, Op. 70, No. 2, last movement (1-8)
Bruckner, *String Quintet in F Major*, last movement (last 17)
Dussek, *Piano Sonatina in F Major*, Op. 20, No. 3, first movement (1-4)
Haydn, *String Quartet*, Op. 33, No. 3, last movement (1-4)
Kuhlau, *Piano Sonatina in G Major*, Op. 88, No. 2, first movement (1-4)
Mozart, *Violin Concerto in D Major*, K. 218, first movement (1-8)
Saint-Saëns, *Sonata for Clarinet with Piano Accompaniment*, Op. 167, first movement (1-3)
Schubert, *Gretchen am Spinnrade* (1-6; last 8)
Tchaikovsky *Symphony VI*, Op. 74, first movement (last 12); second movement (last 7)
Wagner, *Das Rheingold*, "Prelude" (complete); Scene IV, "Entrance of the Gods into
    Walhalla" (1-20; last 15)

2 The V, V$_7$ and V$_9$ Chords

J. S. Bach, *Brandenburg Concerto No. 4*, first movement (1-13)
  Six Little Preludes for Beginners, No. 6 (1-5)
Beethoven, *Für Elise* (1-8)
  Leonore Overture No. 3, Op. 72a, Allegro (1-46)
  Piano Sonatas: Op. 2, No. 3, first movement (1-4); Op. 53, last movement (1-62)
  Sonata for Violin and Piano, Op. 30, No. 3, first movement (1-8); last movement (1-56)
  Symphony III, Op. 55, third movement, Trio (1-32)
  Symphony V, Op. 67, last movement (26-34)
Brahms, *Kinderlieder*, No. 11, "Wiegenlied" (entire)
  Violin Concerto, Op. 77, first movement (1-8)
Chopin, *Berceuse*, Op. 57 (entire)
  Polonaise, Op. 53, E Major portion (5-12)
  Waltzes: in A-flat Major, Op. 69, No. 1 (65-81); in G-flat Major, Op. 70, No. 1 (1-16);
    in D-flat Major, Op. 70, No. 3 (49-56)
Clementi, *Piano Sonatina in C Major*, Op. 36, No. 1, last movement (1-16)
Haydn, *String Quartet*, Op. 33, No. 2, Scherzo, Trio (1-8)
  Symphony in G Major ("Surprise"), No. 94, Menuetto (1-8)
  Symphony in C Major, No. 97, Minuet, Trio (1-16)

* Numbers in parentheses indicate measures.

188

Kuhlau, *Piano Sonatina in C Major,* Op. 55, No. 1, first movement (1-8); last movement (1-16)

Mendelssohn, *A Midsummer Night's Dream,* Op. 61, No. 5, "Intermezzo" (*Allegro molto commodo* to end)
Songs Without Words, Op. 19, No. 3 (1-4)

Mozart, *Piano Sonata in F Major,* K. 332, last movement (15-22)
String Quartet in B-flat Major, K. 458, first movement, at start of Development (1-16)
Symphony in E-flat Major, No. 39, K. 543, Minuet, Trio (1-8)
Violin Concerto in A Major, K. 219, first movement (1-9)

Rossini, *La Gazza Ladra,* "Overture" (1-16)

Schubert, *Impromptu,* Op. 90, No. 4 (1-38)
Waltz, Op. 9a, No. 13 (1-8)
Wiegenlied, Op. 98, No. 2 (entire)

Verdi, *Rigoletto,* Act I, No. 2, "Questa o quella" (1-16)

Weber, *Euryanthe,* "Overture" (1-8)
Invitation to the Dance, Allegro vivace (1-24)

3   The IV Chord

Barber, *Vanessa,* Act II, "Under the Willow Tree" (1-27)

Beethoven, *Overture to Egmont,* Op. 84 (82-89)
Piano Concerto V, Op. 73, first movement (1-8)
Piano Sonata, Op. 79, first movement (1-8)
Seven Country Dances in D Major, No. 7 (complete)
Twelve Variations on the Minuet a la Vigano (theme)

Boccherini, *Cello Concerto in B-flat Major,* last movement (24-31)

Chopin, *Mazurka,* Op. 7, No. 1 (1-12); Op. 17, No. 1 (1-8)
Prélude, Op. 28, No. 10 (6-3 from end)

Haydn, *Piano Trio No. 1 in G Major,* last movement, second subordinate theme (1-8)
String Quartet, Op. 74, No. 3, first movement, second theme of exposition (1-8)

Mendelssohn, *A Midsummer Night's Dream,* "Overture" (1-5)

Mozart, *Piano Sonata in A Major,* K. 331, last movement (coda)

Puccini, *Manon Lescaut,* Act IV, "Sola perduta" (1-37)
Turandot, Act III, Scene 1, "Nessun dorma" (last 4); Act III, Scene 2 (last 7)

Satie, *Gnossienne No. 1* (entire)

Schubert, *Impromptu,* Op. 90, No. 4 (47-56; 88-103)
Piano Sonata, Op. 78, first movement (1-4)
Scherzo in B-flat Major (1-8)
Waltz, Op. 9a, No. 17 (9-16)

Schumann, *Scenes from Childhood,* Op. 15, No. 3 (1-4)

Tchaikovsky, *Symphony V,* Op. 64, last movement (last 20)

Verdi, *La Traviata,* Act I, No. 3, "Libiamo" (introduction and 1-28 of aria)

Wagner, *Das Rheingold,* Scene II (1-8)

4   The Cadential I$^6_4$ Chord

Beethoven, *Piano Sonatas:* Op. 14, No. 2, last movement (1-8); Op. 27, No. 2, last movement, closing theme of recapitulation (1-7)
Symphony I, Op. 21, third movement, Trio (last 16)

Chopin, *Mazurka,* Op. 24, No. 3 (1-13)

Haydn, *String Quartet,* Op. 3, No. 5, last movement (1-8)

Kuhlau, *Piano Sonatina in G Major,* Op. 20, No. 2, first movement (last 22)

Mendelssohn, *Songs Without Words,* Op. 62, No. 4 (1-4); Op. 85, No. 5 (1-5)

Meyerbeer, *Le Prophete,* "Coronation March" (27-34)

Mozart, *An Chloe* (1-8)

Paisiello, *La Molinara,* "Nel cor più non mi sento" (1-8)

Schubert, *Die schöne Müllerin,* Op. 25, No. 12, "Pause" (introduction and postlude)
Octet in F Major, Op. 168, Scherzo (1-8)
Sonatina for Violin and Piano, Op. 137, No. 1, second movement (1-10)
Valses Sentimentales, Op. 50, No. 6 (9-16)

R. Strauss, *Heimliche Aufforderung*, Op. 27, No. 3 (1-8)

Verdi, *Aida*, Act II, Grand March, second theme, "S'intrecci il loto al lauro" (1-8)

5   The II and II₆ Chords

Beethoven, *Piano Concerto IV*, Op. 58, last movement (1-20)
   Piano Sonata, Op. 28, third movement (1-32)
   Sonata for Violin and Piano, Op. 47, second movement (1-16)
   Symphony I, Op. 21, Finale (last 28)
   Variations for Piano Trio, Op. 121a, Variation IX (5-8)
Chopin, *Mazurkas*, Op. 24, No. 2 (13-20); Op. 33, No. 2 (1-48)
Mozart, *Ridente la Calma*, K. 210a (1-6)
   String Quintet in G Minor, K. 516, last movement, Allegro (1-20)
Schubert, *Valses Sentimentales*, Op. 50, No. 13 in A Major
Schumann, *Album for the Young*, Op. 68, No. 10, "The Happy Farmer" (last 4)
J. Strauss, *Morgenblätter Waltzes*, Op. 279, No. 1 (1-16)
Verdi, *Rigoletto*, Act I, No. 3, "Partite? Crudele!" (1-16)

6   The I₆, IV₆ and V₆ Chords

J. S. Bach, *French Suite III*, Minuet (1-5)
Beethoven: *Fidelio*, Act II, No. 16, "Heil sei dem Tag" (introduction 1-32)
   Piano Concerto IV, Op. 58, first movement (1-5)
   Piano Sonata, Op. 2, No. 1, first movement (21-13 from end of recapitulation)
   Symphony V, Op. 67, last movement (1-12); *Symphony VII*, Op. 92, first movement
     (introduction 23-28)
Brahms, *Symphony III*, Op. 90, second movement (1-5)
Buxtehude, *Passacaglia for Organ*, No. 1 (1-8)
Haydn, *Piano Sonatas*: No. 2 in E Minor, second movement (1-8); No. 8 in A-flat Major,
     first movement (1-6); No. 16 in C Major, first movement (1-6)
   String Quartets: in F Major, Op. 3, No. 5, Minuet, Trio (entire) in C Major, Op. 54,
     No. 1, Minuet (1-10)
   Symphonies: No. 97 in C Major, first movement at "Vivace" (1-12); No. 103, in E-flat
     Major, last movement (1-8)
Mendelssohn, *Elijah*, No. 29, "He watching over Israel," chorus (last 8)
Mozart, *Abendempfindung*, K. 523 (1-7)
   Minuet in F Major, K. 2 (1-4)
   Piano Sonata in A Minor, K. 310, first movement (23-35)
   Piano Sonata in F Major, K. 332, first movement (13-22); second movement (1-2)
Rameau, *Gavotte and Variations in A Minor* (theme 1-8)
D. Scarlatti, *Sonata in D Major*, L. 414 (1-7)
Schubert, *Piano Sonata*, Op. 42, third movement (1-5)
   Winterreise, Op. 89, No. 1, "Gute Nacht" (introduction)
Schumann, *Papillons*, Op. 2, Finale (1-19)
Wolf, *Fussreise*, at entrance of voice (1-8)

7   The Inversions of the V₇ Chord

Beethoven, *Piano Concerto I*, Op. 15, first movement, entrance of the piano (1-12)
   Piano Sonatas: Op. 2, No. 1, first movement (1-8); Op. 2, No. 2, second movement (1-8);
     Op. 2, No. 3, second movement (1-4); Op. 10, No. 1, first movement (56-76), second
     movement (1-16); Op. 27, No. 2, second movement, Trio (1-8); Op. 81a, first movement,
     Allegro (5-13); Op. 109, last movement, Variation 1 (1-7)
   Romance in F Major for Violin and Orchestra, Op. 50 (1-8)
   String Quartet, Op. 18, No. 2, third movement (1-8)
   Symphony II, Op. 36, second movement (33-40)
   Trio for Violin, Viola and Cello, Op. 3, first movement (41-48)

Bellini, *La Sonnambula*, Act II, No. 14, "Ah! non credea merarti" (1-11)

Chopin, *Waltzes:* Op. 69, No. 1 (33-48); Op. 69, No. 2 (1-4)

Haydn, *Piano Sonatas:* No. 4 in G Minor, second movement (1-6); No. 5 in C Major, second movement (1-5)
   String Quartet, Op. 20, No. 5, first movement (1-5)
   The Creation, No. 3, "A New Created World," chorus (20-28)

Mendelssohn, *Elijah*, No. 28, "Lift Thine Eyes" (1-8)

Mozart, *Divertimento 1 in D Major*, K. 334, third movement (1-12)
   Phantasie in D Minor, K. 397 (12-15)
   Piano Sonatas: in C Major, K. 279, second movement (1-6); in F Major, K. 280, last movement (1-16); in G Major, K. 283, second movement (1-4)
   Symphonies: No. 36 in C Major, K. 425, second movement (1-12); No. 39 in E-flat Major, K. 543, first movement, Allegro (1-29), last movement (1-16); No. 41 in C Major, K. 551, first movement (1-8), third movement, Trio (1-8)
   The Magic Flute, Act II, No. 20, "Ein Mädchen oder Weibchen" (1-12)
   The Marriage of Figaro, Act III, No. 19, "Dove Sono" (1-18); Act III, No. 20, "Sull' aria" (1-10)

Schubert, *Impromptu*, Op. 90, No. 2 (1-24); Op. 142, No. 2 (1-8)
   Scherzo in B-flat Major, Trio (1-16)

Tchaikovsky, *Pique Dame*, Act II, No. 12, at Andantino mosso (1-8)

Thomas, *Mignon*, Act II, Introduction, "Gavotte" (9-25)

Verdi, *Rigoletto*, Act III, No. 16, "Quartet" (1-8)

8 Six-Four Chords

Section A: Embellishing

Brahms, *Symphony I*, Op. 68, last movement, Allegro non troppo (1-8)

Chopin, *Études*, Op. 10, No. 2 (1-14); Op. 10, No. 5 (1-14)

Clementi, *Piano Sonatinas:* in G Major, Op. 36, No. 5, first movement (1-12); in D Major, Op. 36, No. 6, first movement (1-12)

Haydn, *Piano Sonatina No. 3 in G Major*, last movement (1-8)
   String Quartet, Op. 3, No. 5, second movement (1-12)

Mozart, *Rondo in D Major*, K. 485 (1-16)
   Piano Sonatas: in C Major, K. 330, first movement (1-16, 19-22, 42-58); in C Major, K. 545, first movement (1-4); in B-flat Major, K. anh. 136, last movement (1-16)
   Sonata in C Major for Violin and Piano, K. 296, second movement (1-8)
   Viennese Sonatinas for Piano, No. 1, last movement (1-8); No. 4, first movement (1-8)
   Wiegenlied, K. anh. 284f (entire)

Schubert, *Moment Musical*, Op. 94, No. 2, F-sharp Minor portion (1-6)
   Symphony VII in C Major, first movement, second theme of recapitulation (21-29)

Section B: Passing

Beethoven, *Piano Concerto I*, Op. 15, first movement (1-30)
   Symphony I, Op. 21, second movement (13-26)

Haydn: *Piano Sonatas:* No. 7 in D Major, first movement (1-8); No. 9 in D Major, second movement (21-41); No. 20 in D Major, first movement (17-24)
   Piano Sonatina No. 4 in F Major, last movement (9-16)

Mendelssohn, *Hymn of Praise*, No. 2, "All Men, All Things," chorus (last 10)

Mozart, *Don Giovanni*, Act II, No. 23, "Non mi dir" (1-8 of aria)
   Piano Sonatas: in C Major, K. 330, last movement (1-16); in D Major, K. 311, second movement (1-8)
   Sonata in F Major for Violin and Piano, K. 376, first movement (1-10)

Schubert, *Symphony V in B-flat Major*, first movement (25-40)

Section C: Other Uses

Beethoven, *Piano Sonatina No. 6*, first movement (1-8)
   Piano Trio, Op. 1, No. 2, third movement, Trio (1-10)

Sonata for Cello and Piano, Op. 102, No. 2, first movement (1-8)
  Sonata for Violin and Piano, Op. 24, first movement (38-46)
Handel, *Judas Maccabeus*, No. 7, "O Father, Whose Almighty Power," chorus (1-12)
Haydn, *Piano Sonatina No. 3 in G Major*, last movement (9-16)
Mozart, *Sonata in G Major for Violin and Piano*, K. 301, first movement (1-8)
  Viennese Sonatina for Piano, No. 6, last movement (1-6)
Schumann, *Papillons*, Op. 2, No. 6 (7-14)

9   The VI and VI₆ Chords

J. S. Bach, *Sonata III in E Major for Violin and Clavier*, third movement (1-8)
Beethoven, *Piano Sonata*, Op. 10, No. 3, first movement (87-93)
  Sonata for Violin and Piano, Op. 12, No. 3, last movement (1-8; 56-67)
Brahms, *Intermezzo*, Op. 118, No. 2 (last 10)
Chopin, *Waltz in C-sharp Minor*, Op. 64, No. 2 (33-40)
Dvořák, *Songs of Nature*, Op. 63, No. 4, "Slender Young Birch" (last 8)
Franck, *Prelude, Chorale and Fugue*, "Chorale" (12-15)
Gluck, *Orfeo*, "Dance of the Happy Spirits" (1-8)
Grieg, *Peer Gynt Suite*, "Morning" (1-4)
Handel, *Messiah*, No. 48, "The Trumpet Shall Sound" (entrance of voice 1-16)
Haydn, *Cello Concerto in D Major*, last movement (1-16)
  Piano Sonata in F Major, No. 21, first movement (1-12)
  String Quartet, Op. 54, No. 1, third movement (25-40)
Mendelssohn, *Songs Without Words*, Op. 30, No. 1 (1-5); Op. 38, No. 6 (1-5); Op. 85, No. 6 (1-5)
Mozart, *Eine Kleine Nachtmusik*, K. 525, first movement (1-18); third movement, Trio (1-8); last movement (1-8)
  Piano Sonatas: In F Major, K. 332, first movement (71-76); in B-flat Major, K. 333, last movement (1-20); in C Major, K. 545, last movement (1-8)
  Quintet in A Major for Clarinet and Strings, K. 581, first movement (1-19); last movement (theme)
  Sonata in G Major for Violin and Piano, K. 379, first movement (1-4)
  String Quartet in D Major, K. 575, second movement (1-19)
  Violin Concerto in D Major, K. 218, second movement (last 13)
A. Scarlatti, *O Cessate di Piagarmi* (2-7)
D. Scarlatti, *Sonata in C Major*, Longo S.2 (1-12)
Schubert, *Impromptus*, Op. 90, No. 3 (1-8); Op. 142, No. 2 (17-20; Trio 1-12)
  Piano Sonatas: In A Major, Op. 120, second movement (1-15); in A Minor, Op. 143, second movement (1-4; last 4)
Schumann, *Dichterliebe*, Op. 48, No. 10, "Hör' ich das Liedchen klingen" (1-8)
Tchaikovsky, *1812 Overture* (1-20)
Wagner, *Lohengrin*, Act III (last 11)
  Tannhäuser, Act I, "Dir töne Lob" (1-9)

10   The III and III₆ Chords

Beethoven, *Piano Concerto V*, Op. 73, second movement (16-26)
Brahms, *Magelone Lieder*, Op. 33, No. 4, "Liebe kam aus fernen Landen" (1-6)
  Romance, Op. 118, No. 5 (1-4)
Chopin, *Mazurka*, Op. 68, No. 3 (9-16)
Dvořák, *Symphonies*, No. 8, Op. 88, third movement, Trio (1-18); No. 9, Op. 95, third movement, Trio I (1-31); last movement (10-25)
Handel, *Messiah*, No. 12, "For Unto Us a Child Is Born" (12-18)
Liszt, *Piano Concerto I in E-flat Major*, last movement (entrance of piano, 1-5)
MacDowell, *Woodland Sketches*, Op. 51, No. 1, "To a Wild Rose" (1-8)
Moussorgsky, *Pictures at an Exhibition*, "The Great Gate at Kiev" (1-22)
Mozart, *String Quartet in E-flat Major*, K. 428, Menuetto (27-34)
  Symphony in D Major, K. 504, first movement, Allegro (30-35)
Rachmaninoff, *Nocturne*, Op. 10, No. 1, Trio (1-7)

Schubert, *Impromptu*, Op. 90, No. 4 (72-79)

Tchaikovsky, *Nutcracker Suite,* "Marche" (last 8)

Verdi, *Rigoletto,* Act I, "Introduction," Allegro con brio (1-8)

Wagner, *Lohengrin,* Act 1, Scene III, "Nie sollst du mich befragen" (1-8); Act III, "Treulich geführt" (Wedding March, 1-16 of chorus)

    Siegfried, Act III, Scene 3, "Heil dir Sonne!" (1-16)

Wolf, *Tretet ein, Hoher Krieger* (last 4)

11   The VII and VII₆ Chords

Beethoven, *Piano Sonata,* Op. 49, No. 1, first movement (1-8)

Brahms, *A German Requiem,* Op. 45, No. 11, "Now, therefore, be patient" (at C, 1-9)

Gluck, *Alceste,* "Caprice" (1-8)

    Orfeo, Act III, No. 42, "Che farò senza Euridice" (1-10)

Handel, *Messiah,* No. 42, "Hallelujah Chorus" (1-4 of chorus; at C, "The kingdom of this world," 1-8)

    Verdi Prati (piano introduction and 1-8 of voice)

Haydn, *Piano Sonatas:* No. 12 in G Major, third movement (17-24); No. 15 in D Major, third movement (1-10)

    String Quartet, Op. 17, No. 5, second movement (21-32)

Mozart, *Allegro in B-flat Major,* K. 3 (last 10)

    Piano Sonatas: in B-flat Major, K. 281, first movement (1-8); in G Major, K. 283, first movement, development section (1-9)

Saint-Saëns, *Sonata for Clarinet with Piano Accompaniment,* Op. 167, third movement (26-32; last 8)

Schumann, *Album for the Young,* Op. 68, No. 2, "Soldiers March" (last 8)

    Dichterliebe, Op. 48, No. 3, "Die Rose, die Lilie" (1-8)

12   Successive First Inversions

Beethoven, *Trio for two Oboes and English Horn,* Op. 87, Finale (1-16)

Bellini, *La Sonnambula,* Act III, No. 14, "Ah! non credei" (11-19)

Haydn, *Piano Sonatas:* No. 5 in C Major, first movement (45-61); No. 8 in A-flat Major, last movement (24-14 from end)

Mendelssohn, *Elijah,* No. 28, "Lift Thine Eyes" (last 12)

Mozart, *Piano Concerto in F Major,* K. 459, second movement (62-74)

    Piano Quartet in G Minor, K. 478, last movement (9-16)

    Piano Sonata in G Major, K. 283, first movement (last 16); last movement (1-24)

    The Magic Flute, Act II, No. 9, "March of the Priests" (1-4)

    The Marriage of Figaro, Act III, No. 19, "Dove Sono" (9-18)

13   Sequence

Beethoven, *Piano Sonata in G Major,* Op. 79, third movement (1-4)

    Piano Trio in C Minor, Op. 1, No. 3, Finale (212-216)

Chopin, *Mazurka in F Major,* Op. 68, No. 3 (1-16)

Haydn, *String Quartet,* Op. 17, No. 2, second movement (21-32)

Kuhlau, *Piano Sonatina in A Minor,* Op. 88, No. 3, last movement (55-71)

Mozart, *Piano Sonata in C Major,* K. 545, last movement (1-8)

    Symphony No. 38 in D Major, K. 504, first movement, Allegro (19-27)

    The Magic Flute, Act I, No. 5, Andante, "Drei Knäbchen, jung, schön" (1-12); Act II, No. 12, Quintet, "Wie? wie? wie?" (1-8)

14   The II₇ Chord and Its Inversions

J. S. Bach, *Sonata II in E-flat Major,* for Flute and Harpsichord, second movement (1-4)

    The Well-Tempered Clavier I, "Prelude I" (1-4)

Beethoven, *Piano Concerto I,* Op. 15, second movement (1-8)

Piano Sonatas: Op. 2, No. 3, first movement (1-13); Op. 10, No. 2, second movement, Trio (1-8); Op. 28, second movement (1-4); Op. 31, No. 3, first movement (1-17)
  Symphony IX, Op. 125, third movement (3-12)
Berlioz, *Roman Carnival Overture,* Op. 9 (at English Horn solo, Andante sostenuto, 1-8)
Bizet, *Symphony I,* second movement (9-20)
Brahms, *Auf dem Schiffe,* Op. 97, No. 2 (entrance of voice, 1-8)
  A German Requiem, Op. 45, No. 3, "Lord make me to know" (2-33)
  Symphony IV, Op. 98, third movement (last 11)
  Trio in C Major, Op. 87, second movement (1-8)
Chopin, *Étude,* Op. 25, No. 11 (last 4)
  Nocturne in C-sharp Minor, Op. Posthumous (5-12)
  Waltzes: in C-sharp Minor, Op. 64, No. 2 (33-40); in A-flat Major, Op. 70, No. 2 (1-8); in E Minor, Op. Posthumous (9-24)
Dvořák, *Symphony IX,* Op. 95, second movement (7-21; last 18)
Franck, *Prelude, Fugue and Variation for Organ,* Op. 18, "Variation" (7-12)
Gounod, *The Redemption,* Part III, No. 1, "Lovely Appear," at entrance of soprano (1-12)
Grieg, *Peer Gynt Suite,* "Ase's Death" (1-4)
Handel, *Messiah,* No. 3, "Every Valley" (aria 1-10)
Haydn, *Symphony No. 103 in E-flat Major,* Menuetto (1-10)
Kuhlau, *Piano Sonatina in A Minor,* Op. 88, No. 3, first movement (1-8)
Mendelssohn, *Violin Concerto,* Op. 64, first movement (1-10)
Mozart, *Ave Verum,* K. 618 (1-8)
  Der Zauberer (1-4)
  (Little) Fantasia in F Minor for Organ, at Allegro (1-4)
  Piano Sonatas: in F Major, K. 280, second movement (1-8); in A Minor, K. 310, second movement (1-8); in B-flat Major, K. anh. 136, Menuetto, Trio (1-8)
  Symphonies: No. 39 in E-flat Major, K. 543, last movement (1-30); No. 41 in C Major, K. 551, last movement (1-8)
Rachmaninoff, *In the Silent Night,* Op. 4, No. 3 (last 7)
Schubert, *Schwanengesang,* No. 5, "Aufenthalt" (1-14)
  Sonatina for Violin and Piano, Op. 137, No. 3, last movement (9-16)
  Viola, Op. 123, at entrance of voice (1-12)
Schumann, *Dichterliebe,* Op. 48, No. 5, "Ich will meine Seele tauchen" (1-4)
  String Quartet in A Major, Op. 41, No. 3, first movement (1-15); last movement (1-4)

15   The VII₇ Chord and Its Inversions

J. S. Bach, *Twelve Little Preludes,* No. 3 in C Minor (1-7)
Brahms, *Symphony III,* Op. 90, third movement (1-8)
Haydn, *Piano Sonatas:* No. 12 in G Major, second movement, Trio (last 8); No. 20 in D Major, second movement (1-4)
Mozart, *Piano Sonata in C Minor,* K. 457, first movement (1-19); last movement (1-4)
Schubert, *Symphony V,* third movement (1-18)
Verdi, *Aida,* Act II, "Ah! pietà ti prenda" (1-9)

16   Other Seventh Chords

Bach, *Christmas Oratorio,* No. 41, " 'Tis Thee I would be praising" (1-3)
  Little Prelude and Fugue in B-flat Major, for Organ, "Fugue" (last 9)
  The Well-Tempered Clavier I, "Prelude in C-sharp Minor" (1-10); "Prelude in G Major" (last 4); "Prelude in G Minor" (9-12)
Beethoven, *Piano Sonata,* Op. 109, second movement (1-8)
Brahms, *Ballade,* Op. 118, No. 3 (15-17)
Debussy, *Ballade in F Major* (6-10)
Handel, *Messiah,* No. 5, "Thus saith the Lord" (15-22)
Medtner, *Novelette,* Op. 17, No. 1 (1-9)
Monteverdi, *Ariana,* "Lasciatemi morire!" (1-6)
Mozart, *Piano Sonata in F Major,* K. 332, first movement (34-24 from end)
Philipp, *Pastels,* Op. 24, No. 3, "Feux-Follets" (45-53)

Ravel, *Pavane* (1-12)

A. Scarlatti, *Le Violette* (last 10)

Schubert, *Fantasia,* Op. 15, first movement (11-13)

17 Secondary Dominants

Section A: of V

Beethoven, *Piano Sonata,* Op. 2, No. 2, third movement (1-8)
 Sonata for Violin and Piano, Op. 12, No. 1, last movement (1-8)
 Symphony IX, Op. 125, third movement (1-19)

Brahms, *Liebeslieder,* Op. 52, No. 10 (1-10)
 Vergebliches Ständchen, Op. 84, No. 4 (1-20)

Chopin, *Ballade in G Minor,* Op. 23 (9-12)

Haydn, *String Quartets:* in D Minor, Op. 76, No. 2, second movement (1-4); in B-flat
 Major, Op. 76, No. 4, third movement (1-8); in D Major, Op. 76, No. 5, second movement (1-9)

Mozart, *Don Giovanni,* Act I, No. 7, "Là ci darem la mano" (1-8)
 Piano Concerto in A Major, K. 488, first movement (31-46)
 Piano Sonata in D Major, K. 311, last movement (1-16)
 Trios: in G Major, K. 496, second movement (1-8), third movement (1-8); in G Major,
 K. 564, last movement (1-8)

Schubert, *Impromptu in B-flat Major,* Op. 142, No. 3 (1-8)
 Winterreise, Op. 89, No. 5, "Der Lindenbaum," entrance of voice (1-16)

Schumann, *Fantasiestücke,* Op. 12, No. 3, "Warum" (1-4)

Wagner, *Tannhäuser,* "Overture" (1-8)

Section B: of IV

J. S. Bach, *Two-Part Invention No. 14 in B-flat Major* (1-5)

Beethoven, *Piano Sonatas:* Op. 10, No. 2, first movement (1-12); Op. 10, No. 3, second
 movement (1-9); Op. 28, first movement (1-39; last 50); Op. 53, last movement (last 8);
 Op. 110, last movement (10-14)
 Piano Sonatina No. 1 in G Major, second movement (1-8)
 Symphony I, Op. 21, first movement, introduction (1-12)

Brahms, *Der Schmied,* Op. 19, No. 4
 Liebeslieder, Op. 52, No. 9 (1-15)

Chopin, *Piano Concerto I in E Minor,* Op. 11, second movement at entrance of piano
 (1-10)
 Prélude in G Major, Op. 28, No. 3
 Waltz in A Minor, Op. 34, No. 2 (17-36)

Handel, *Messiah,* No. 20, "He Shall Feed His Flock," Introduction (1-4)

Haydn, *Piano Trio No. 7 in E Minor,* first movement (35-44)

Mendelssohn, *Midsummer Night's Dream,* Op. 61, "Nocturne" (1-16)
 Songs Without Words, Op. 53, No. 1 (1-11)

Schubert, *Moment Musicale,* Op. 94, No. 3 (1-10)
 Waltzes, Op. 9a, No. 11; Op. 9b, No. 3; Op. 50, No. 2 (9-16)

Schumann, *Myrthen,* Op. 25, No. 1, "Widmung" (1-13)
 Quintet in E-flat Major, Op. 44, second movement (1-10)

Tartini, *Violin Sonata in G Minor* ("The Devil's Trill"), last movement, at Grave in D
 Minor (1-6)

Tchaikovsky, *Piano Concerto in B-flat Minor,* Op. 22, second movement (5-12)

Weber, *Der Freischütz,* "Overture" (9-25)

Wieniawski, *Violin Concerto in D Minor,* Op. 22, second movement (1-8)

Section C: of II

Beethoven, *Piano Sonatas:* Op. 2, No. 3, second movement (1-11); Op. 10, No. 3, third
 movement (1-16); Op. 13, second movement (1-16); Op. 81a, third movement (11-17)
 Rondo in G Major, Op. 51, No. 2 (17-24)
 Symphony I, Op. 21, first movement, Allegro con brio (1-21)

Bellini, *Norma,* Act I, No. 4, "Casta Diva," at entrance of voice (1-8)

Berlioz, *Les Nuits d'été,* Op. 7, No. 4, "Absence" (1-15)

Chopin, *Nocturne in E Major,* Op. 62, No. 2 (1-8)
  Prélude, Op. 28, No. 7 (entire)
Haydn, *Quartet,* Op. 76, No. 4, first movement (1-12); second movement (1-8)
Mendelssohn, *Songs Without Words:* Op. 53, No. 4 (1-9); Op. 62, No. 6 (1-15); Op. 102, No. 7 (7-22)
Mozart, *Piano Sonatas:* in B-flat Major, K. 281, last movement (1-8); in C Major, K. 309, last movement (1-19); in D Major, K. 576, first movement (1-8)
Purcell, *Dido and Aeneas,* Act I, No. 6, "Fear no danger," chorus (1-8)
Schubert, *Octet,* Op. 166, last movement (1-16)
  Symphony V, last movement (1-16)
  Viola, Op. 123, entrance of voice (1-12)
Schumann, *Arabeske,* Op. 18 (1-16)
  Der Abendstern, Op. 79, No. 1 (entire)

Section D: of VI

J. S. Bach, *Eight Little Preludes and Fugues for Organ,* "Prelude IV in F Major" (1-14)
Beethoven, *Piano Sonatas:* Op. 2, No. 1, last movement, transition to recapitulation (1-18); Op. 10, No. 3, last movement (1-9); Op. 28, first movement (63-70); Op. 106, second movement (1-7)
  Sonata for Violin and Piano, Op. 96, second movement (1-8)
  String Quartet, Op. 18, No. 2, second movement (1-6)
  The Ruins of Athens, "Turkish March" (1-28)
Brahms, *Variations on a Theme by Haydn,* Op. 56a (1-10)
Chopin, *Étude,* Op. 10, No. 3 (last 16)
Haydn, *The Creation,* No. 3, "A new created world," chorus (29-37)
Mendelssohn, *Songs Without Words,* Op. 19, No. 4 (6-13)
Saint-Saëns, *Samson et Dalila,* Act II, "Ah! résponds à ma tendresse" (1-21)
Schubert, *Ecossaise,* Op. 18a, Nos. 1 and 3
  Impromptu in A-flat Major, Op. 142, No. 2 (9-16)
  Piano Sonata in A Major, Op. 120, last movement (11-19)
  Waltzes, Op. 9a, Nos. 1 and 3
  Wanderer's Nachtlied, Op. 4, No. 3 (1-4)
  Winterreise, Op. 89, No. 19, "Täuschung" (1-21)
Schumann, *Dichterliebe,* Op. 48, No. 14, "Allnächtlich im Traume" (last 12)
  Fantasiestücke, Op. 12, No. 4, "Grillen" (1-16)
  Myrthen, Op. 25, No. 3, "Der Nussbaum" (1-6)
  Nachtstücke, Op. 23, No. 4 (1-10)
  Papillons, Op. 2, No. 1 (1-8)
Verdi, *Rigoletto,* Act III, No. 15, "La donna è mobile" (1-16)

Section E: of III

Beethoven, *Piano Concerto IV,* Op. 58, second movement (1-13)
  Piano Sonatas: Op. 2, No. 1, last movement (1-9); Op. 81a, last movement (20-12 from end)
  Sonata for Cello and Piano, Op. 69, second movement (1-16)
  The Ruins of Athens, "Turkish March" (entire)
Chopin, *Mazurka,* Op. 67, No. 2 (1-16)
  Nocturne, Op. 37, No. 1 (1-8)
  Polonaise, Op. 40, No. 1, D major section (1-8)
Handel, *Messiah,* No. 6, "But who may abide the day of His coming?" (introduction, 1-12); No. 36, "Thou art gone up on high" (introduction, 1-11)
Mendelssohn, *Songs Without Words,* Op. 62, No. 5 (1-12); Op. 102, No. 3 (43-55)
Schumann, *Album for the Young,* Op. 68, No. 6, "The Poor Orphan" (1-8)

Section F: of VII

Beethoven, *Piano Sonata,* Op. 28, second movement (17-22)
Brahms, *Ballade,* Op. 118, No. 3 (1-10)
Corelli, *La Folia* (9-16)
Schumann, *Märchenbilder,* Op. 113, No. 2 (51-58)

18 Diminished Seventh Chords: Dominant Function

Section A: of V

J. S. Bach, *Prelude and Fugue in F Minor,* for organ, "Prelude" (last 13)
   Well-Tempered Clavier I, "Prelude V" (last 11)
   Well-Tempered Clavier II, "Prelude XII" (1-4)

Beethoven, *Piano Sonatas:* Op. 2, No. 1, first movement (41-48); Op. 31, No. 3, first movement (1-8); Op. 81a, second movement (1-8)
   Quartet, Op. 18, No. 1, second movement (1-8)
   Wonne der Wehmut, Op. 83 (last 8)

Brahms, *Therese,* Op. 86, No. 1, introduction (1-5)

Chopin, *Maiden's Wish* (entire)

Donizetti, *L'Elisir d'Amore,* Act II, Scene 8, "Una furtiva lagrima" (entrance of voice, 1-8)

Haydn, *Quartet,* Op. 76, No. 4, first movement (1-22)

Mendelssohn, *Songs Without Words:* Op. 19, No. 2 (1-8); Op. 85, No. 6 (1-5)
   Symphony III, Op. 56, first movement (1-8); third movement (1-29); last movement (23-11 from end)

Schubert, *Impromptu in B-flat Major,* Op. 142, No. 3 (1-8)

Tchaikovsky, *Symphony V,* Op. 64, third movement (1-8)
   Symphony VI, Op. 74, first movement (20-23)

Verdi, *La Forza del Destino,* Act III, "Oh, tu che in seno" (1-8)

Wagner, *Tannhäuser,* Act III, "O du mein holder Abendstern" (1-8)

Section B: of IV

J. S. Bach, *English Suite IV,* "Sarabande" (13-16)
   Partita VI in E Minor, "Toccata" (17-20)
   Well-Tempered Clavier II, "Prelude XII" (last 5)

Beethoven, *Trio in C Minor,* Op. 1, No. 3, last movement (314-328)

Mozart, *Piano Quartet in G Minor,* K. 478, first movement (last 28)
   Piano Sonata in C Minor, K. 457, third movement (228-248)
   String Quartet in C Major, K. 465, last movement (257-272)

Schumann, *An den Mond,* Op. 95, No. 2 (Introduction)
   Arabesque, Op. 18 (57-64)
   Der arme Peter, Op. 53, No. 3b (last 8)
   Piano Concerto in A Minor, Op. 54, first movement (32-35)

Tchaikovsky, *Symphony V,* Op. 64, first movement, introduction (1-10)

Section C: of II

Beethoven, *Piano Sonata,* Op. 7, third movement (25-42)

Chopin, *Nocturne in E-flat Major,* Op. 9, No. 2 (1-4)
   Waltz in E-flat Major, Op. 18 (1-18)

Haydn, *Symphony No. 97 in C Major,* first movement, introduction (1-14)

Mozart, *Fantasia in F Minor,* for organ, K. 608, Andante (1-8)
   The Magic Flute, Act I, No. 8, "Könnte jeder brave Mann" (1-8)

Schubert, *Piano Sonata in A Major,* Op. 120, first movement (1-8)
   Symphony V, last movement (1-16)

Schumann, *String Quartet in A Minor,* Op. 41, No. 1, second movement, Intermezzo section (1-16)
   Symphony I, Op. 38, second movement (1-23)
   Symphony III, Op. 97, third movement (1-5)
   Variations on the name "Abegg," Op. 1, Theme (1-16)

Section D: of VI

Beethoven, *Piano Sonata,* Op. 31, No. 2, second movement (1-18)
   String Quartet, Op. 18, No. 2, first movement, second theme of recapitulation (1-8)
   Trio, Op. 1, No. 3, second movement, coda (1-12)

Haydn, *Quartet,* Op. 76, No. 4, second movement (1-16)

Mendelssohn, *Elijah,* No. 43, "And then shall your light break forth" (last 15)

Mozart, *Piano Quartet in G Minor,* K. 478, second movement (1-19)

Quintet in A Major for Clarinet and Strings, K. 581, second movement (1-20)
String Quartets: in D Minor, K. 421, second movement (15-26); in B-flat Major, K. 458, second movement (1-8)
Symphony in C Major, K. 551, second movement (1-11)
Schubert, An die Musik, Op. 88, No. 4 (1-19)
Schumann, Myrthen, Op. 25, No. 1, "Was will die einsame Thräne?" (last 14)
Verdi, La Traviata, Act II, No. 10, "Di provenza il mar" (entire)

Section E: of III

Mendelssohn, Andante Cantabile e Presto Agitato in B Major, for piano (last 18)
Mozart, Piano Sonata in F Major, K. 280, first movement (13-26)
Schumann, Nachtstüke, Op. 23, No. 2 (1-4)
Symphony I, Op. 38, third movement (last 33)
Tchaikovsky, Nutcracker Suite, "Dance of the Reed Flutes" (11-18)

19 Diminished Seventh Chords: Non-Dominant Function

Beethoven, Sonata for Violin and Piano in G Major, Op. 96, second movement (1-8)
Quartets: Op. 18, No. 3, second movement (1-12); Op. 74, second movement (1-9)
Brahms, Quintet in F Minor, Op. 34, Finale (41-53)
Symphony IV, Op. 98, last movement (var. 26)
Trio in C Major, Op. 87, Finale (1-11)
Violin Concerto, Op. 77, first movement (136-164)
Chopin, Grand Valse brillante, Op. 18 (29-36)
Franck, Symphony in D Minor, second movement (17-32)
Grieg, Lyric Pieces, Book III, Op. 43, No. 1, "Papillon" (last 9)
Mendelssohn, Piano Concerto in G Minor, Op. 25, Finale (40-47)
Songs Without Words, Op. 67, No. 6 (1-27)
Mozart, Quartet in E-flat Major, K. 428, first movement (12-24)
Schubert, Quintet in A Major, Op. 114, first movement (26-38)
Quintet in C Major, Op. 163, first movement (1-20)
Trio, Op. 99, last movement (1-26)
Schumann, Carnaval, Op. 9, No. 2, "Pierrot" (1-8)
Der arme Peter, Op. 53, No. 3a, "Der Hans und die Grete" (1-18)
Piano Sonata in G Minor, Op. 22, second movement (1-11)
Tchaikovsky, Symphony VI, Op. 74, first movement (89-97)
Verdi, Aida, Act II, finale, "Gloria all' Egitto, ad Iside" (1-10)
La Forza del Destino, Act III, "Oh, tu che in seno agli angeli" (8-4 from end)
Wagner, Tannhäuser, Overture, at Allegro (30-39)
Weber, Piano Sonata in E Minor, Op. 70, second movement (1-24)

20 Modulation to the Dominant Key (Major Mode)

J. S. Bach, Brandenburg Concerto No. 4, first movement (1-35)
English Suite IV, "Sarabande" (1-8)
French Suites: IV, "Sarabande" (1-8); "Minuet" (1-8); V, "Gavotte" (1-8); VI, "Gavotte" (1-8); "Minuet" (1-8)
Little Notebook for Anna Magdalena Bach, No. 15, "March in D Major"
Two-Part Inventions: No. 1 in C Major (1-7); No. 8 in F Major (1-12)
Beethoven, Minuet in G (entire)
Piano Sonatas: Op. 2, No. 2, last movement (1-8); Op. 14, No. 2, second movement, Trio (1-16); Op. 28, second movement, Trio (1-8); Op. 79, last movement (1-8)
Quartet, Op. 18, No. 5, third movement (1-16)
Rondo in G Major, Op. 51, No. 2 (1-24)
Six Easy Variations in G Major, theme (1-8)
Sonata for Violin and Piano, Op. 30, No. 2, second movement (1-8); third movement (1-18)
Symphonies: I, Op. 21, third movement, Trio (1-24); II, Op. 36, first movement (73-98)
Thirty-three Variations on a Waltz by Diabelli, Op. 120, theme (1-16)
Boccherini, String Quintet in A Major, "Minuet" (1-8)